HOW DEAF CHILDREN LEARN

Marc Marschark
Patricia Elizabeth Spencer

The World of Deaf Infants: A Longitudinal Study
Kathryn P. Meadow-Orlans, Patricia Elizabeth Spencer, and
Lynn Sanford Koester

Sign Language Interpreting and Interpreter Education:
Directions for Research and Practice
Edited by Marc Marschark, Rico Peterson, and Elizabeth A. Winston

Advances in the Sign Language Development of Deaf Children
Edited by Brenda Schick, Marc Marschark, and Patricia Elizabeth Spencer

Advances in the Spoken Language Development of Deaf and Hard-of-Hearing Children
Edited by Patricia Elizabeth Spencer and Marc Marschark

The Gestural Origin of Language
David F. Armstrong and Sherman E. Wilcox

Deaf Cognition: Foundations and Outcomes
Edited by Marc Marschark and Peter C. Hauser

A Lens on Deaf Identities
Irene W. Leigh

The People of the Eye: Deaf Ethnicity and Ancestry
Harlan Lane, Richard Pillard, and Ulf Hedberg

How Deaf Children Learn: What Parents and Teachers Need to Know
Marc Marschark and Peter C. Hauser

How Deaf Children Learn

WHAT PARENTS AND TEACHERS NEED TO KNOW

Marc Marschark

and

Peter C. Hauser

OXFORD
UNIVERSITY PRESS

OXFORD
UNIVERSITY PRESS

Oxford University Press, Inc., publishes works that further Oxford University's objective of excellence in research, scholarship, and education.

Oxford   New York
Auckland   Cape Town   Dar es Salaam   Hong Kong   Karachi   Kuala Lumpur   Madrid   Melbourne
Mexico City   Nairobi   New Delhi   Shanghai   Taipei   Toronto

With offices in
Argentina   Austria   Brazil   Chile   Czech Republic   France   Greece   Guatemala   Hungary   Italy
Japan   Poland   Portugal   Singapore   South Korea   Switzerland   Thailand   Turkey   Ukraine
Vietnam

Published by Oxford University Press, Inc.
198 Madison Avenue, New York, New York 10016

www.oup.com
Oxford is a registered trademark of Oxford University Press

Library of Congress Cataloging-in-Publication Data

Marschark, Marc.
How deaf children learn : what parents and teachers need to know / Marc Marschark Peter C. Hauser.
p. cm.
Includes bibliographical references and index.
ISBN 978-0-19-538975-3
1. Deaf children—Means of communication. 2. Deaf children—Language. 3. Deaf—Education.
4. Parents of deaf children. I. Hauser, Peter C. II. Title.
HV2391.M257 2012
371.91'2—dc22
2011012553

---

9 8 7 6 5 4 3 2

Printed in the United States of America on acid-free paper

In memory of Cyril Courtin
Friend, Scholar, Hero

Contents

HOW DEAF CHILDREN LEARN

1

WHAT IT'S ALL ABOUT

TO BEGIN WITH, we should point out that writing this book was not our idea. It was not something that we even dreamed of before we hosted a conference in 2006 at the National Technical Institute for the Deaf on "Cognitive Underpinnings of Learning by Deaf and Hard-of-Hearing Students." Supported by the National Science Foundation, the conference brought together researchers from around the world to shed some light on how deaf and hard-of-hearing students learn and, in particular, how we can support their learning. People who read the resulting book, *Deaf Cognition: Foundations and Outcomes* (Oxford, 2008), found it interesting and thought provoking, but they pointed out that while useful for researchers, it was a little too "dense" for readers outside of psychology and educational research.[1] At the suggestion of editors at Oxford University Press and people whom we thought were our friends, we therefore decided to try to translate that book from "researchese" into English suitable for lay readers. Honestly, we thought that it would be easier than it turned out to be.

As we will describe in the chapters that follow, the education of deaf and hard-of-hearing children has long been guided as much or more by intuition as evidence. The earlier book, however, described work by experts in the fields of education, cognitive science, literacy, and child development that seemed likely to have implications for parents and teachers of deaf children. That's a good thing, too, because research, legislation, and social change in many countries recently have led to a

focus on the effectiveness and efficiency (including the economics) of educational methods both with regard to children in general and especially in special education. *Special education*, in the sense used here, usually refers to the need to modify instructional methods or materials used with the majority of children in particular ways to be accessible or effective with subgroups of children seen as having special needs. Most of the studies described in the earlier book did not specifically include such modifications, but they revealed characteristics of deaf learners that told us a lot about how they learn—and why they sometimes do not learn as much as we (and they) think they do.

The case of deaf children in special education raises two unique issues. One issue, which we will address at various places throughout this book, is the belief of many people that except for differences in hearing and sometimes in the *modality* of their language (spoken versus signed), deaf children and hearing children are just the same. From that perspective, if we remove communication barriers in the classroom through sign language, cochlear implants, or other technologies, the two groups should learn the same material at the same rate in the same ways. But they don't. And, as you will see, research shows this assumption is wrong.

The second issue is that unlike other subgroups of children with special education needs, deaf children are often seen as part of a *linguistic-cultural minority*. That is, they are part of a community that shares a language, culture, values, and a view of the world that in many ways is different from the hearing majority. Yet because 95% of deaf children are born to hearing parents, they do not start out as card-carrying members of that linguistic-cultural group, and some never will be.

Regardless of whether any particular deaf child grows up to be a member of that group, seeing deaf people in a linguistic-cultural light has led to research in psychology, language, and education that has identified *strengths* as well as *needs* of children and older students who are deaf or hard of hearing. To the extent that those studies have produced consistent and explainable results, they support our view of the first issue, that is, that deaf children may not be simply hearing children who can't hear. More to the point, we believe that all of this says that if we want to give deaf children opportunities for successful academic outcomes, we need to better understand who they are, what they know, and how they think. That is what this book is all about.

WHO ARE WE AND WHAT ARE WE DOING HERE?

We suggested earlier that we thought this book would be easier to write than it turned out to be. There are two different elements to this. First, throughout the book we offer specific suggestions to parents and teachers about educating deaf children, based on the available evidence. However, we were able to do so less often than we might have wished. For the most part, this is because—as we emphasize throughout the book—most of the questions about educating deaf children are quite complex, and they do not have simple answers. We do make general recommendations and sometimes offer specific advice about ways to support deaf children's development and activities that promote their learning at home and in the classroom. All of these are suggestions for *evidence-based practice*, that is, educational practice based on the existing research literature. In most areas, however, we found that existing research evidence was insufficient for us to be able to suggest that readers do one thing rather than another. We were afraid that at best, that road would give parents and teachers a false sense of security and perhaps prevent them from looking beyond this very basic examination of how deaf children learn. At worst, we could be as overly simplistic and misleading as some of the unfounded claims in the field we are trying to debunk.

The second reason why this book turned out to be harder to write than we expected relates to another point we will emphasize repeatedly, that individual differences among deaf and hard-of-hearing children are greater than they are among hearing children. Particularly when multiple challenges are involved, but even when they are not, deaf children differ from each other in all of the ways that hearing children do *plus* in the quality and quantity of early language they receive (see Chapter 4); the breadth of their experience interacting with people and things in the world (see Chapter 5); and possible physical, psychological, or brain-related issues associated with the medical or hereditary causes of their hearing status (see Chapter 3). For this reason, too, we felt that dispensing too much advice without the support of research would be dangerous.

If it seems that we are being somewhat conservative in all this, the reader should recognize that both of the authors are psychologists, teachers, and researchers, and thus have ethical obligations at several different levels. In addition, as will become evident later, there also is a fair bit of political sensitivity in the field of deaf education that demands that we tread carefully if we want to change the way that people see and teach deaf children. All of this was captured in a National Public Radio (*Talk of the Nation*) interview sometime back with author Malcolm Gladwell. First, he said "We've been arguing about this question for hundreds of years now, and we're at a point in the argument, I'm afraid to say, where evidence isn't changing people's minds at all." Second, he noted that "If you are scientist . . . you have an obligation when you speak to speak carefully . . . and produce the evidence to back up what you say."

In fact, Gladwell was talking about possible relations between race and intelligence, but he might just as easily have been talking about language choice or school placement with regard to deaf children. Both issues have been argued about for hundreds of years and, to a large extent, evidence is not changing people's minds about either. At the same time, as we suggested earlier, one reason why minds are not being changed is that there are people in the field—some of them highly respected—who are making claims (and being believed) without the evidence to back up what they say. Our primary goal in this book is to provide parents and teachers with objective, evidence-based information about educating deaf children. If we can change some minds along the way, all the better.

ALTERNATIVE PERSPECTIVES ON EDUCATING DEAF STUDENTS

A number of years ago, before we had much of the evidence described in this book, one of us suggested that there appeared to be two broad approaches to education and to the education of deaf and hard-of-hearing children, in particular. One approach to classroom instruction, generally acknowledged in the field of education, was called the *hydraulic model* of education. The hydraulic model views information and knowledge like a fluid that has to be transferred from the head of the teacher to the head of the child. The good news is that because all children's heads are about the same, when we fill them, the fluid will conform to any minor differences in shape. The hard part is figuring out the most effective way to transfer the fluid, especially to deaf children. Do we try to pour it in as quickly as possible or a bit at a time (that is, give them a lot of practice all at once or space practice out over time)? Do we warm it up first (that is, simplify it) so that it feels more comfortable? What is the best container/pouring system (that is, language) to use? How can we be sure it fills up all the little nooks and crannies without leaving gaps?

Teachers who favor the hydraulic model appear to believe that more information is better, which may be why many of them like the Internet so much: It offers immediate access to a huge amount of information. Educational researchers who (implicitly or explicitly) accept the hydraulic model see child development in the same way as they see education: the process of effectively transferring knowledge and skills from the environment and from others to the child through teaching, trial-and-error learning, and by experimentation. *Maturation* (natural growth) provides increasing space for storing information in this model; thus, cognitive development, language development, and social development proceed at much the same rate for most children across different cultures and contexts.

Consistent with the hydraulic view of development and education, several researchers have argued that many of the cognitive changes we see in children as they grow up are more the result of changes in they way the process information than from increasing knowledge. As young children develop greater attention and memory ability, for example, they are better able to deal with information of cognitive, linguistic, and social importance. In other words, the shape of the learning container may change over time, but it does so in gradual, predictable ways.

In contrast to the information transmission approach of the hydraulic model, other teachers adopt what looks like more of a *water park model* of education. In this view, there is no single, simple description of knowledge or knowledge acquisition. Information is "out there" in the world in a variety of forms, it can be accessed in a variety of ways, and no two children will do exactly the same things or react in exactly the same ways. The water park model assumes that children all have somewhat different learning styles and slightly different learning needs, at least for optimal learning. All of this variation comes from differences in early experiences, skills, and the brain—including language, the functioning of our senses (or not), and everything that is learned right up to the moment.

Viewed from the water park, deaf and hard-of-hearing children are likely to have different and more diverse learning styles and needs than hearing children. Both between-group differences (deaf versus hearing) and within-group differences (deaf and hard of hearing) mainly are a result of differences in children's early environments, a topic to be considered in several of the following chapters. Adding to the normal, background differences among deaf children, however, will be differences related to the causes of their hearing loss and early experience compared to hearing peers.

From the point of view of teachers and researchers, all of this makes life difficult. Not only do we have to find the most effective way to support learning in deaf and hard-of-hearing children as a group, but each child may learn differently and at a different rate. For the most part, such differences may be small and perhaps even irrelevant in a classroom. Sometimes, for some children, they will be critical.

Since we first offered that description, over 10 years ago, both our own research and research of others in the field has supported it from both the student and the teacher points of view. For example, as we will describe later, we have now shown that teachers in hearing classrooms are more likely to adhere to the hydraulic model, whereas experienced teachers of the deaf are more likely to view education according to the water park model. Presumably, this is the result of their experience and not anything that they were taught which led them to teach hearing or deaf students in the first place. Deaf and hearing children, too, will be shown to have somewhat different approaches to learning, although in their case, these seem to be the result of experience and the way in which they are educated. The following chapters, therefore, will disentangle ways in which experience affects education and ways in which education can influence experience. Together, we believe that these will help to explain why deaf and hard-of-hearing children sometimes struggle in school and what we can do about it.

USING THIS BOOK

The following chapters describe what we see as the basic building blocks underlying learning by deaf and hard-of-hearing children. Each of them will be an important piece of the educational success puzzle. Taken together, they will give a clearer picture of what we know about deaf and hard-of-hearing children's development and how it fits (or not) with the teaching-learning of hearing children both in the classroom and in informal settings. Hopefully, we have provided this information in a way that is relatively easy to digest. For those who want more in-depth or technical information about the various topics, Suggestions for Further Reading are provided at the back of the book.

We strongly suggest that this book be read chapter by chapter, in the order each appears. This is not to keep you from reading bits and pieces while having coffee in the bookstore, but because many of the chapters build on earlier ones both conceptually and in terminology. To give you a brief overview, Chapters 2–5 provide general information about how it is that some children are born or become deaf, about deaf people and deaf education, and about hearing and hearing loss (including hearing aids and cochlear implants). While Chapters 2 and 3 deal with what it means to be deaf in a hearing-oriented world, Chapter 4 describes alternative methods of communication used by and with deaf children, cognitive and educational implications of them, and some of the sticky language issues that have created debate in the field for generations. Chapter 5 looks inside families with a deaf child. It includes some of the practical issues parents encounter in raising a deaf child and also the social and cognitive foundations of learning that develop at home, before a deaf child ever steps foot in a school. This is also the place where we first begin to see differences between deaf and hearing children that will have continuing (and sometimes increasing) effects on development and education.

Chapters 6–8 in many ways are the "meat" of this book, focusing on cognition and cognitive development of deaf and hard-of-hearing children, that is, everything that goes into *learning*. They include discussions of intelligence, memory, problem solving, and several other aspects of cognition and learning that we will explain as we go along. Our emphasis on the subject matter in these chapters, like our emphasis on communication and language, it is not because we are researchers who study cognition and language (although we are). Just the opposite: We are interested in these areas precisely because we see them as the essence of what humans are all about. If we don't understand the language and cognitive environments and abilities of deaf children, or if we assume that they are identical to those of hearing children, we will never be able to help deaf children to reach their full potential. Thus, it is in these chapters where we will see differences between deaf and hearing learners, some of which we have known about for a long time, even if we only recently have come to recognize their importance for academic achievement.

Chapters 9–11 address three major aspects of schooling and school success. Chapter 9 deals with *print literacy*, or reading and writing—what traditionally has been seen as the greatest academic hurdle for deaf students (although some recent research of our own suggests that this might not be the case). Chapter 10 considers mathematics, usually seen as the second-biggest hurdle for deaf students. In part, this is because of the way that mathematics is given such a central place in education—quite appropriately in our view. Just as important, however, we will see that most of the research concerning the education of deaf and hard-of-hearing children has focused on reading and mathematics, with relatively little attention given to other areas of the curriculum. Chapter 11 looks at the classroom itself, including teachers and the other people who play important roles in educating deaf children. Finally, Chapter 12 looks at the larger context of differences between deaf and hearing students, and how we can take advantage of those differences rather than using them as excuses. In this chapter, we also look ahead to what we believe can be a much brighter future for deaf education and for the lives of deaf learners of all ages.

NOTES, CONFESSIONS, AND ACKNOWLEDGMENTS

Portions of this book were drawn from previous books by the authors, but Oxford University Press doesn't mind. Photo and art credits (and our appreciation) go to Mark Benjamin, Linda Burik, Erin Campion, Peter C. Hauser, Jorge Samper, and W. T. Greenough. We also thank Lou Abbate, Sue Archbold, Erin Campion, Catharine Carlin, Gerry O'Donoghue, Risa Pegler, Cathy and Don Rhoten, Lawrence Scott, Jr., Patricia E. Spencer, and the members of the Center for Education Research Partnerships for their contributions to this book, regardless of whether they realize it. Perhaps most important, we thank Sarah L. Harrington, our editor at Oxford University Press, for her patience, her comments on an earlier version of this book, and, once again, for her patience. Preparation of this book was supported in part by grants REC-0814332 (MM) and SBE-0541953 (PH) from the National Science Foundation. Any opinions, findings and conclusions, or recommendations expressed in this material are those of the authors and do not necessarily reflect the views of the National Science Foundation.

2

INTRODUCTION TO DEAF CHILDREN

PERHAPS IT GOES without saying that all children are different and all families are different. All parents experience joys and difficulties in raising their children, and there is no such thing as the "perfect child." Nevertheless, the more different any particular child is from others of his age and sociocultural group, the more likely it is that his parents will face a variety of practical challenges and sometimes have to make decisions on the basis of less information than they might want. Teachers often face similar situations with either one or two students who have special needs or, as communities become more diverse, a classroom full of differing backgrounds and abilities. For parents and teachers who unexpectedly find themselves with a deaf or hard-of-hearing child, this book is for you. But where do we start?

It is not difficult to find descriptions of some parents' experiences of shock and grief when they discover that they have a deaf or hard-of-hearing child, but how individual parents respond varies greatly. Certainly, it would be an understatement to say that some emotional and practical "adjustments" are necessary in such situations. Nevertheless, adjustments do occur and most deaf and hard-of-hearing children grow up to be just as well behaved, happy, and intelligent as their hearing peers. During the first few months and years, however, their parents often struggle as they try to figure out what kind of early intervention services provide the best fit for their child and the family, how best to interact with their child in order to ensure a strong emotional bond, and what mode of communication is best. For some,

these issues feel more like, "She's deaf? What do I do now?" "I'm afraid I'm going to do the wrong thing!" and "Sign language? You mean [waving hands wildly in the air] that?" Before they know it, parents are faced with the question of what school setting will best support their child's strengths and needs: A regular local classroom? A school for the deaf? A separate classroom in a public school? By this point most parents are walking, talking experts on deaf children.

For the teachers who encounter a deaf child in their classrooms for the first time, there is also likely some anxiety at first (which seems more professional than saying "they freak out"). There already is not enough time in the school day, not enough resources, and as many social-behavioral problems as can possibly be handled by a single human being. As with the parents of a deaf child, teachers may look to a book or two about special education or about educating deaf children, but to misquote a movie character, there are "too many words." The classroom issues seem overwhelming—from sign language to hearing aids and from reading difficulties to captioned videos. Often, all of this eventually boils down to figuring out how to work with a *sign language interpreter* or an *itinerant teacher of the deaf* (see Chapter 11), someone who provides varying levels of support for deaf students in a number of different schools ("Eek! Another adult in my classroom?"). Some accommodations are easily accomplished, like rearranging the classroom to improve acoustics and ensuring that the deaf student can see the teacher's face at all times ("I'm supposed to remember that?"). Other issues, like restructuring the way information is presented (see Chapters 6 and 8) and learning to deal with hearing-related classroom technologies systems, take more getting used to.

Most centrally, both parents and teachers need to focus on the importance of effective communication. Along with that focus, however, will come the tacit assumption that once communication barriers are removed, deaf children will learn just like hearing children. That is the sentiment expressed in most of the books they read and what they find on the Internet, and it makes intuitive sense. Unfortunately, it is to a large extent wrong.

For those looking for simple solutions, we frequently have to caution, as we noted in Chapter 1, that deaf children are not just hearing children who can't hear. Research has shown that their knowledge, cognitive abilities, and learning styles (see Chapters 6–8) are somewhat different than those of hearing children of the same age. That is both good news and bad news. The bad news, of course, is that some teaching methods and materials are going to have to change, just as parents have to develop different methods of social interaction and informal instruction in the home. The good news is that now that we have discovered these differences, we should be able to create settings in which deaf children succeed just as readily as their hearing classmates. Indeed, high expectations and recognizing the unique strengths and needs of deaf students are what it's all about. Otherwise, we will not be able to provide them with the quality education that is morally and legally their right.

NAVIGATING ISSUES

Even a brief look at the literature about raising and educating deaf children will reveal another challenge for parents and teachers, one that we will try to avoid in the following pages. To be blunt, in this field, opinions and personal beliefs often get in the way of facts. This is a particular problem because the field is strongly split on several different issues of importance. Consider the two most frequently encountered examples. First, *the language question*. We have known for over 50 years that American Sign Language (ASL) and other natural sign languages are true languages, just like English or Spanish. (In Chapter 4 we discuss the difference between natural sign languages and the artificial sign systems frequently used in schools.) We also have known for a long time that sign language *does not* interfere

with deaf children's learning to speak. If anything, early sign language has beneficial effects on learning spoken language for children with and without cochlear
implants (see Chapters 3 and 4). The evidence also indicates that exposing a deaf
child only to spoken language usually results in language delays from early childhood continuing at least through the high school years. Yet advocates of spoken
language for deaf children only rarely concede these facts.

Similarly, advocates of bilingual education for deaf children (e.g., ASL and
English) have not yet demonstrated that children in those programs become fluent
in both languages . . . or either one. They continue to claim that sign language is
the answer to deaf children's academic challenges, but we are still waiting to see
evidence to support that claim. As we will see, the fact that deaf children of deaf
parents usually have full access to language from birth, through their parents' signing, does provide them with advantages in social-emotional development as well as
language development. In contrast, the claim that because they learn sign language
early, those children do better in school than deaf children who have hearing parents is not as well established as many would have us believe. It appears to be early
access to language, not the modality of that language, that is important.

Our goal here is not to determine which approach is right and which is wrong.
Rather, everyone needs to understand that there is no "one-size-fits-all" answer to
the language question. If we are going to make decisions about raising and educating deaf children, they should be made on the basis of the available evidence and
the needs and strengths of each child.

Second, consider *the cochlear implant issue*. We discuss implants more in the next
chapter, but if you are reading a book about deaf children, you probably already
have a rough idea of what implants are all about. Again, however, you are more
likely to have encountered opinions and politics on the issue—both for and
against—than facts. As much as implants have helped many deaf children improve
their hearing, language, and academic achievement, they are not a "cure for deafness." The typical child with an implant hears about as well as his hard-of-hearing
grandfather. Just like grandpa, he will pick up more in one-on-one conversations
than in noisy settings like classrooms and will be more likely to understand people
on the telephone if he knows them than if he does not. This is not to deny the
potential benefits of implants; it is simply to point out that they do not turn deaf
children into hearing children (see Box 2.1). We will see later that implants are not
for everyone, but those children who have them generally do better in school than
other deaf children. Nevertheless, most still face challenges not encountered by
their hearing peers.

If these two examples seem disheartening, it is important to note that great
progress has been made over the last 25 years in our understanding of language
and learning by children who are deaf (unfortunately, much less is known about

BOX 2.1
QUESTIONS AND ANSWERS FROM
HTTP://WWW.EDUCATINGDEAFCHILDREN.ORG

Question: Is there any evidence that providing exposure to sign language to cochlear implanted children could hinder speech development?

Answer: Actually, the research is very clear that sign language *does not* hinder speech development in children with cochlear implants . . . in fact, it may facilitate it. Research from the Nottingham Cochlear Implant Centre has shown that 3 years after cochlear implantation, deaf children's spoken language skills are independent of whether they started out signing or utilizing spoken language only. With regard to language after receiving an implant, research has shown that parents and children move toward spoken language after implantation, at least to the extent that it works for the child. When it doesn't, parents and children (appropriately) move toward sign language. There are a couple of older studies which indicated that deaf children with cochlear implants who were in "oral" settings had better spoken language than others in total communication settings. However, those studies were done back when the children who received implants were the ones who already were showing particular facility for spoken language, and there is no recent evidence to support that view. In general, sign language can be acquired earlier than spoken language, and it may provide a "framework" for early spoken language development. Future research will have to answer that question but, in the meantime, there is no evidence that sign language in any way has negative effects for children or young adults with cochlear implants.

those who are hard of hearing). Deaf people have never before had as much access to education and employment, and we have never been in a better position to overcome the remaining barriers facing deaf children. At the same time, as we noted earlier, every child is different, every family is different, and every classroom is different, too. As a result, for every general research finding described in this book, someone will be able to offer an exception (either positive or negative). Nevertheless, there is enough good information available to provide parents and teachers with guidance in educating deaf children.

We understand that some even well-informed decisions will be difficult, and some likely will turn out to be wrong. What is important is that decisions and action plans be made only when all of the options are known and are made on the basis of real evidence rather than unsupported (if appealing) claims. For that reason, the descriptions and discussions you will encounter in the following chapters are based on research findings that we believe can be trusted, and we will warn you when relevant studies have been misinterpreted or have not yet been done.

In addition to controversies, there is also a lot of broad agreement in raising and educating deaf children. Most notably, there is universal agreement that early intervention and effective parent–child communication early on are powerful predictors of success in essentially all areas of deaf children's development, including education. Many parents thus learn sign language in order to communicate with their deaf child at an earlier age even if they do not sign well. Other parents find that their children do well with spoken language even if they do not speak quite like their hearing siblings and need to work very hard at listening. As we will see, full and early access to language, whatever its form, is the most important foundation for success. Regular monitoring of a child's language progress therefore is essential, as is a willingness to make changes in programming if the child is not achieving her full potential.

Unfortunately, some of the available research on language choices for deaf children is not very helpful. It often applies only to *some* deaf children in *some* situations and all too often authors' conclusions do not follow from their results. This situation is partly due to the great variability among deaf children across essentially all areas of development. In the following chapters, we will see the effects on both language development and academic achievement of medical issues, communication fluencies, early environments, social interactions, and differences in access to sound. These contributing factors often are not considered by researchers, either because they focus only on one group—perhaps deaf children with cochlear implants or those who have deaf parents—or because there are not enough children in their studies to "control" for these factors.[1]

We also have to admit that some of the weakness in language research involving deaf children results from conscious or unconscious bias on the part of investigators who often seem only to obtain (or publish) findings that support their own positions. Other times such research reflects a lack of appropriate research methods or training; or the research may just be old and based on incomplete knowledge compared to what we know today. In describing deaf children's learning, clearly indicating both what we know and what we do not know, we will focus on the abilities that support their educational success. Language will find its way into most of these discussions because of its importance to all aspects of child development and education. However, we will only separate spoken language and sign language when their effects are known to be different. Most of the time, it is *language* that matters, not whether it comes from the mouth or the hands.

THOSE WHO IGNORE HISTORY. . .

It is often said that "those who ignore history are doomed to repeat it," and yet there is also the expression that "the more things change, the more they stay the same."

Both can be true, of course, and to those interested in educating deaf children, it seems they often are. For those of us with experience in the field, these expressions serve as a reminder that where we are today in understanding and supporting the educations of deaf children is a direct result of a self-made history. Decisions (sometimes by omission—deciding not to act) made in the field over the past 200 years have influenced the lives of countless deaf children. Now we find ourselves at another decision point, with an opportunity to take advantage of recent advances in psychological and educational research, technology, and improved teaching practices, and fundamentally change the way we approach the education of deaf children.

The Changing Face of Deaf Education

Over the past century or so, the education of deaf children has changed dramatically in the number of children it reaches, its content, and where it happens. From 1850 to 1950, enrollment in residential schools for the deaf and other special programs in the United States rose from just over 1,100 to over 20,000. By the early 1970s, that number had more than tripled, largely due to the rubella (German measles) epidemic of 1962–1965. By the mid-1970s, over a third of all deaf children attended special schools, and another third attended special programs within regular schools. Since that time, however, the number of children in schools for the deaf has decreased dramatically, especially at the elementary school level. According to recent U.S. government data, only about 12% of deaf children are now educated in separate schools,[2] and over 86% are in regular school classrooms for at least part of the school day.

Perhaps more than where they are educated, the most dramatic changes in the education of deaf children have been the introduction of sign language into the classroom and the movement away from an emphasis on vocational training toward the same academic curriculum offered to hearing children. Many countries have passed laws guaranteeing appropriate educational opportunities for all children, regardless of their hearing status. Those laws are sometimes misinterpreted, or perhaps we should say that they have been interpreted in different ways that often leave parents and educators frustrated. Current laws in the United States require early identification of hearing losses in school-age children, unbiased evaluation of deaf children using a variety of alternative communication methods, and free and appropriate public education. Similar laws exist in many other countries.

In the United States, these laws came about because only about half of all children with disabilities attending public schools were receiving the support necessary for even low-level academic success, and over 1 million disabled students were excluded from public school classrooms altogether! Although the laws do not

always describe exactly what educational options must be provided for children with disabilities, in the United States, they require *(1)* that all children from age 3 to 21 years be educated "in the least restrictive environment" (LRE) as close as possible to a child's home, *(2)* the availability of a range of places in which education can occur, and *(3)* the development of individualized education programs (IEPs) for each child with special educational needs. They also require that parents be included in decision making about educational issues affecting their disabled children.

The primary source of confusion and consternation in all of this concerns the definition of "least restrictive environment" and the intent of the requirement that "disabled" children should be educated with "nondisabled children" to the maximum extent possible. The goal of the U.S. legislation was to stop discrimination in education that prevented children who were viewed as disabled from attending schools and programs where they could function successfully. Unfortunately, the law was not clear on whether putting children into regular classrooms was a requirement or an option. Nor is it always clear whether a regular classroom is more or less restrictive for a deaf child compared to a separate classroom (think "access to language"). Dr. Lou Abbate, executive director of the Willie Ross School for the Deaf (which includes *partnership classrooms* in local public schools) has suggested that "the most enabling environment" would be a more appropriate requirement, arguing that "the least restrictive environment is not a place, it is a service to be provided."

The LRE issue has become more important in the United States since passage of the No Child Left Behind Act (NCLB) in 2001, which required greater accountability on the part of schools to ensure *adequate yearly progress* of their students. One interesting and unexpected consequence of NCLB is that some deaf children who have not done well in public schools are now being shifted to schools and programs for the deaf. Unfortunately, those transfers sometimes seem more designed for the benefit of the public school than the child—so a low-performing deaf child will not pull down school test scores. Not only does the public school have a higher test score average as a result, but the school for the deaf is receiving a child who is already behind grade level and thus may obtain lower achievement scores. Parents and state education officials thus should use caution in interpreting the test scores of both local schools and schools for the deaf when it comes to placing deaf children.

In contrast to the aforementioned situation, the evidence suggests that schools and programs specifically designed for deaf children often may be more academically appropriate for them than general education programs. In recent years, there also has been an increasing movement of deaf teens (with and without cochlear implants) from their local public schools to special programs for social-emotional reasons. Let's face it: Teens are not always accepting and supportive of others who are different. Some deaf students want to be with others who are like them, a particularly important issue when they are developing their own senses of identity.

Much of the controversy surrounding educational placement for deaf children in the United States should have been eliminated by clarifications to previous legislation provided by the Department of Education in 1992. The Department listed five considerations that school districts and state education departments are required to take into account in determining school placements and IEPs for deaf children:

- Language needs
- Severity of hearing loss and potential for using any remaining hearing with or without amplification devices (hearing aids, FM systems, etc.)
- Level of academic skills
- Social, emotional, and cultural needs, including opportunities for interaction and communication with peers
- Communication needs, including the child's and the family's preferred mode of communication.

Questions remain, however, about how to make sure that deaf children and school systems have the resources necessary for educational success and how teaching in a regular classroom can be adapted to meet the strengths and needs of deaf and hard-of-hearing children. To the extent that those children do not always learn in the same ways as hearing children, the methods and structure of the regular classroom may not be to their greatest advantage without specific modifications. And that is what much of this book is all about.

TERMS OF ENDEARMENT (OR NOT)

To fully appreciate where we are in educating deaf and hard-of-hearing children—and where we still need to go—it will help to clarify some basic terminology. The general term *hearing impaired* is one that is used frequently to refer to people with any amount of hearing loss, although it is used less frequently in the United States than elsewhere. In 1991, a joint statement by the World Federation of the Deaf and the International Federation of Hard of Hearing People rejected the term *hearing impaired* as "pathology oriented," indicating a preference for the general term *deaf and hard of hearing*. Nevertheless, *hearing impaired* remains popular in countries such as the United Kingdom and Australia, where it is sometimes synonymous with *hard of hearing*.

What, then, exactly is meant by *deaf*? Hearing losses are not all-or-none. There is a continuum of hearing loss from those so subtle that they might not be noticed to losses so severe that hearing aids and other amplification devices are essentially worthless (see Chapter 3 for details on all of this). Even the term *loss* is not always appropriate, because some children are born deaf (they did not have a chance to lose anything). In this book, we will use the term *deaf* in the sense of having less access to sound and therefore depending more on vision. Interestingly, however, there is no legal definition of deafness comparable to the legal definition for blindness. For convenience, we also will sometimes use the term *hearing loss*, despite its inappropriateness and negative connotation.

Hard of hearing is a term frequently encountered in reference to hearing status. To most people, "hard-of-hearing people" are those like our parents or grandparents who simply do not hear quite as much as they used to. Hard-of-hearing children frequently have good speech in addition to more hearing than deaf children. The problem is that teachers often wrongly assume that because a hard-of-hearing child speaks clearly, she also hears well. As a result, hard-of-hearing children are often reported to "fall between the cracks" and not receive the support they need in classrooms composed primarily of hearing children. Recent studies have shown that even when their hearing is only slightly below normal, children are at risk academically, suggesting that both deaf and hard-of-hearing children would benefit from many of the same support services. Unfortunately and perhaps surprisingly, less is known about hard-of-hearing children's academic foundations and outcomes than about deaf children, even though there are far more of them. This may be the result of the considerable variability among hard-of-hearing children (see Chapter 3) and thus the difficulty of identifying factors that predict their developmental and academic progress. Because many deaf children with cochlear implants function like hard-of-hearing children, we expect that more research focusing on these children will be forthcoming in the near future.

Then there is the issue of *deaf* versus *Deaf*. Although *deaf* is sometimes used as a generic adjective, many people now limit its use to the audiological sense, referring only to lack of hearing. "Big D deaf" is used in the sociocultural sense, referring to individuals who see themselves as part of a community bound together by history and by sign language. References both to the Deaf community and to Deaf culture thus are typically written in the capitalized form. The Deaf community is rich in art, humor, and literature, in addition to sharing most of those enjoyed by hearing people. In this sense, being Deaf can offer children the same kind of cultural diversity available in the United States to African American, Hispanic, or Jewish families who can appreciate mainstream American culture while also having a link to a special heritage. While Deaf people usually identify themselves as users of a natural sign language (e.g., American Sign Language [ASL], Sign Language of the Netherlands [NGT]), very little is known about how or when language and cultural orientations affect deaf children's self-identities or academic achievement.

Another distinction we have to make concerns the general term *sign language* and more specific terms like *sign systems* and *natural sign languages* like ASL (see Chapter 4). For the most part, we will use *sign language* to refer to any language that makes primary use of the hands and face to communicate grammatically through visual-spatial means. *Sign systems* essentially combine two languages, like using the grammar of English and the signs of ASL. In addition, sign and speech together—called *simultaneous communication* in the United States and *sign-supported speech* in some other countries—are frequently used at home and in the classroom. Contrary to various claims, there is no research evidence showing that these combined systems do deaf children any good or any harm. At the very least, they may be easier for hearing adults to learn, because it is not necessary to learn an entirely new grammar.

In contrast to created sign systems, natural sign languages like ASL, used in the United States and in English-speaking parts of Canada (Langue des Signes Québécoise [LSQ] is used in French-speaking Canada) are true languages according to linguistic definitions. There is no universal sign language any more than there is a universal spoken language.

DIFFERENCES VERSUS DEFICIENCIES

Family doctors usually deal with hearing children. The frequency of severe to profound hearing loss in the general population is so low that most pediatricians encounter deaf children only rarely, if ever. Moreover, *congenital* (from birth) and *early-onset* (in the first year or two) hearing losses often are not easily noticed unless one is looking for them. When physicians do encounter young children with serious hearing losses, they tend to view them in terms of the pathology model acquired during their medical school training ("hearing loss as illness"). From that perspective, being deaf is considered a serious handicap and a barrier to normal development. True, being deaf deprives children of some of the experiences available to normally hearing children, like the enjoyment of music or the sound of oncoming cars, although hearing aids and cochlear implants can give many deaf children some access to these. Other experiences simply may be different than when children are hearing, like the rules of children's games or the way they learn to read. Anyone who has ever watched a basketball game between two deaf schools and the enthusiasm fostered by their cheerleaders, however, knows that some things are always the same.

The experiences of children who differ in their hearing status will affect how they view and interact with the world in a variety of subtle and not-so-subtle ways. This *interactive* and *cumulative* nature and development is shown in Figure 2.1. In the case of deaf children of deaf parents, the greater range of language-related and social experiences compared to deaf children of hearing parents leads to their passing through most developmental stages at the same rate as hearing children. For deaf children of hearing parents, less effective communication with their parents means that explanations of events are often incomplete or absent. As a result, those experiences also may not blend so readily into the background of family and community life. For them, experiences may be more limited or atypical because of

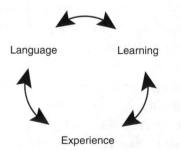

FIGURE 2.1 Language, learning, and experience influence and build on each other.

parental overprotection (see Chapter 5) and thus are more likely to lead to differences in their social, language, and perhaps their cognitive functioning compared to hearing children. But wait, there's more!

Our primary reason for emphasizing differences between deaf and hearing children at this point is a practical one. There is an understandable tendency on the part of many of us to deny or minimize handicaps that are not visible. Indeed, it is easier for most people to recognize and accept the obstacles faced by a child in a wheelchair than by one with a learning disability, or by a child who is blind than by one who is deaf. But denying a child's hearing status or any other possible barrier to full access, no matter how stress reducing to parents or grandparents in the short run, does no one any good in the long run. Eventually, overlooking children's difficulties catches up with them, with their parents, and with society. Sometimes the realization comes too late; it always comes at a higher cost.

As we noted earlier, the necessity of early language is an assumption that guides most of our thinking about the normal development of all children. For centuries, philosophers and scientists have tried to understand the relation between language and thinking, oversimplifying the issue to "Does language depend on thought, or does thought depend on language?" This debate was a particularly popular scientific pastime during the 18th and 19th centuries, with deaf individuals being used as examples on both sides of the argument. We now know that the language we use does not *determine* the way we think, but the languages that children learn and the context in which they learn them will affect the way that they view the world.[3] For example, a child may never have met a Crustacean, but if her parents repeatedly tell her that Crustaceans look funny, smell funny, and walk funny (and they would not want a Crustacean to move in next door), the child is likely to develop a prejudice against Crustaceans.

Similarly, as shown in Figure 2.1, it is not just explicit teaching in the classroom that requires and contributes to fluency in language. The vast majority of most children's informal experiences come in the form of language or are at least accompanied by language. Our perceptions and conceptions of the world will be colored just as much by the way something is described as by its factual content (like those crabby Crustaceans). Much of a young child's experience thus will be shaped by the language of parents and teachers who are communicating with a particular purpose in mind. It does not matter much if they are using English, Japanese, or ASL—the content and effects of that communication are always present. Therefore, if a child does not have age-appropriate access to language, an essential component of development will be missing.

We believe the stage is now set to begin discussing where, when, and how deaf and hard-of-hearing children learn and what we can do to support that learning.

First, a note of clarification: Although we used the term *deaf and hard-of-hearing children* in the previous sentence, we have already acknowledged that less is known about hard-of-hearing children than about deaf children. In the next chapter, we will see some of the reasons for this situation, the result of the great variability in hard-of-hearing children's hearing sensitivity, and the causes of their hearing losses. These differences make research with that population difficult. Fortunately, a large multisite research project is underway in the United States in an effort to better understand the implications of mild to moderate hearing loss (see Chapter 3) in children. In the following chapters, we refer to "deaf children" in a general sense to mean both deaf and hard-of-hearing children in contexts where the issues are generally the same for children with less than full hearing. Where necessary, we will distinguish subgroups within that larger population.

FINAL WORDS

In most respects, deaf and hearing children are essentially the same. Like hearing children, deaf children's success begins with acceptance and communication at home. Attention to their special needs acknowledges that deaf children may be different from hearing peers, but those differences should not be taken to mean that deaf children are defective or deficient. Instead, it is essential that we recognize that deaf children vary greatly—just like hearing children—and we have to treat them as individuals. Optimizing their opportunities in school and the social world requires a more complete understanding of deaf people and related issues than most hearing people have. The remainder of this book therefore will provide a survey of what we currently know about how language, social, and intellectual development of deaf children influence academic outcomes and how we can best support their educational endeavors. First, we will consider the senses of hearing and vision and what it means for deaf children to be living primarily in a visual world.

3

ON HEARING AND NOT HEARING

IT IS DIFFICULT to deny that a child who cannot hear or cannot see will be somewhat different than a child who has all five senses. Certainly, there will be some obvious differences in behavior, such as not noticing people who are trying to get their attention by calling to them or waving, respectively. There are also going to be more subtle differences, like what they know about different animals or what makes people smile. In order to know whether such differences are likely to affect academic achievement, and thus enable adults to appropriately modify instructional methods if necessary (or helpful), we have to know what those differences are. In the case of deaf and hard-of-hearing children, we know that their brains develop differently than the brains of hearing children because of the lack of *audition* (hearing), their greater reliance on vision, and related differences in experience. This chapter therefore provides a summary of what we know about these issues in children and how they might affect formal and informal learning.

UNDERSTANDING HEARING

Sometimes, when audiologists or doctors talk to parents about their children, they sound like they are speaking in mathematics. Parents usually want to know how much their deaf child can hear, if any at all, but it is important to consider *what as* well as *how much* the child can hear. We therefore will describe first how the medical profession classifies different hearing levels and then a bit about hearing and hearing loss. Having a general understanding of all this can help parents and teachers talk about children's hearing and related needs while also helping them to understand when research is relevant or irrelevant to a specific deaf or hard-of-hearing child.

The perception of sound varies both in *loudness* and in *pitch* or *frequency*. The decibel (dB) is the common unit of measurement for the intensity of sounds, perceived as loudness. For example, the loudness of normal speech in an otherwise quiet environment is about 60–65 dB. The music of rock bands begins at about 85–90 dB and goes up to 115 dB. This volume is 10% louder than a jackhammer, and many of our more senior rock musicians now have significant hearing losses. Traveling in a car at 55 miles per hour, with the windows rolled up, air conditioning and heat off, and no one talking produces background noise of about 80 dB. NASCAR drivers, in contrast, are constantly bombarded with noise up to 100 dB and more, perhaps explaining why some appear to have hearing losses and affection for loud country music. Equally loud automobile noise also can be caused by three children, a puppy, and a radio in an air-conditioned car on the way to the beach. Luckily, that noise does not last long, and its effects are only temporary.

When a child's hearing is tested, the measurement of most practical interest is the *pure tone hearing threshold in the better ear*. This is essentially how loud sound has to be to be heard. Hearing levels usually are described in terms of a *PTA* or *pure tone average*, the average threshold or how loud sound has to be across all sound frequencies to be heard. For children with greater hearing thresholds (that is, greater hearing losses) already present at birth or appearing soon after, the frequencies of their thresholds can vary widely, with a wide range of possible implications. This caution is especially important for hard-of-hearing children because the patterns of their frequency thresholds tend to vary the most. The hearing losses most frequently seen in older adults, in contrast, usually affect the ability to hear sounds at higher frequencies. This explains why your grandfather often can hear his (male) friends' voices but not your grandmother's (even if she thinks he does it on purpose!).

Hearing is considered normal with thresholds up to 25 dB in the better ear, although recent research indicates that thresholds as low as 16 dB can create academic challenges for children. Thresholds from 26 to 40 dB are referred to as *mild* hearing losses, those from 41 to 55 dB as *moderate,* and those from 56 to 70 dB as *moderately severe*. Hearing thresholds from 71 to 90 dB are associated with *severe* hearing losses, and those over 91 dB are considered *profound* (see Table 3.1). Once again, however, loudness or intensity is not the only factor affecting whether we can hear speech, because the particular frequency of a sound makes a big difference in

TABLE 3.1

Hearing thresholds and descriptive labels	
Intensity of Sound (dB)	Hearing Level
Up to 25 dB	Normal
26–40 dB	Mild hearing loss
41–55 dB	Moderate hearing loss
56–70 dB	Moderately severe hearing loss
71–90 dB	Severe hearing loss
>91 dB	Profound hearing loss

what is heard. Normally, humans can hear sounds in the range of 20 to 20,000 hertz (Hz, the standard measure of frequency). Dogs can hear sounds over 30,000 Hz, the range of "silent" dog whistles, which are too high pitched for us to hear. When it comes to human speech, losses that affect hearing in the range of 500 to 2000 Hz are those that are most troublesome, because those are the frequencies at which the important features of spoken language are expressed. (We will see later that hearing a word is not the same as being able to understand it.)

Approximately 1 in 1,000 infants is born with a hearing threshold greater than or equal to 35 dB in the better ear. *Bilateral* hearing losses (in both ears) occur about once in every 750 births. This rate of *congenital* (from birth) hearing loss plus the frequency of acquired hearing losses suggests there may be more than 100,000 children in the United States with reduced hearing sensitivity, and more than 70,000 have thresholds that qualify them for special education services. The situation is surely more varied and complex elsewhere. Australian Aboriginal children, for example, are both prone to middle ear infections (*otitis media*) and often live in remote areas where medical treatment and antibiotics are in short supply. As a result, 25%–30% have significant hearing losses. Similar numbers have been suggested by colleagues working with Inuit children in northern Canada.

Imagine blowing across the top of an open 2-liter soda bottle filled with water or, better yet, try it out (if you can hear). When the bottle is half filled with water, it will make a higher pitched sound than blowing into an empty container. When there is water in the bottle, the vibrations created in the bottle neck do not have as much room to expand in the smaller areas, resulting in shorter wavelengths and thus higher frequency sounds. Similarly, the shorter vocal cords and smaller chest volumes of most children and females compared to adult males usually make their voices higher in frequency.

Types of Hearing Loss

When illness, accident, or genetics (heredity) reduce the amount of hearing a child has, the resulting losses usually can be categorized as *conductive* or *sensorineural*. Conductive hearing losses are those that affect transmission of vibrations through the ear. Usually, the damage is to either the eardrum or the small bones of the middle ear (the hammer, anvil, and stirrup). Conductive losses also can include blockage of the ear canal with wax or fluid. Most often, conductive hearing losses result from severe or repeated ear infections that inflame and damage the eardrum or the bones of the middle ear. Ear infections account for over 10 million visits to the family doctor each year in the United States. Many children have repeated ear infections that can temporarily damage their eardrums and their hearing, and otitis media is one of the most common causes of hearing loss seen in children after infancy.

Sensorineural hearing losses typically involve the cochlea or its connections to the auditory nerve, which runs to the brain. Such losses reduce or eliminate the nerve impulses that represent sound, so people with such hearing losses cannot even hear their own voices. As will be described later, it is here that cochlear implants have their primary benefit.

Causes of Hearing Loss

The causes (or *etiologies*) of reduced hearing sensitivity in children vary widely and can result from maternal or fetal illness prior to birth, illnesses during childhood, or from hereditary (genetic) factors. The most frequent causes of childhood hearing loss today are premature birth and genetics. Only 25% of deaf children come from families with histories of hearing loss, but about 80% of the cases of elevated hearing thresholds in childhood have a genetic component. Genetic effects on hearing can be either *acute* (beginning all at once) or *progressive* (increasing over time). Progressive hearing losses may not be detectable at the time of newborn hearing screening.

The variety of causes of hearing losses in children contributes to the differences that we see in their development. Hearing losses linked to illness or accidents carry the risk of damage to other sensory systems or of related neurological effects, and one-third of all types of hereditary deafness also have associated medical or physical implications. Approximately half of children with *cytomegalovirus* (CMV), a virus that affects brain tissue, have multiple disabilities in addition to being deaf. Premature birth also sometimes is associated with disabilities beyond hearing loss, including a higher frequency of behavioral problems, delays in language and cognitive development, and delays in physical development and coordination.

Various estimates suggest that 30%–40% of all deaf children have psychological, neurological, or physical conditions related to their hearing losses, whether or not they are obvious or affect behavior. Reports of psychological or behavioral differences between deaf and hearing children need to be considered with some caution, however. A characteristic that might be described as "due to deafness" might really be the result of something else, most likely a brain-related factor. In short, because deaf children vary so widely and for so many reasons, it is important that their needs be evaluated carefully so we can offer them the best environments for growth and learning.

HEARING AIDS

When a hearing loss affects only the intensity of sound perception, amplification often can improve hearing. However, loss of intensity usually is not the same across all frequencies, and as we have already noted, higher frequencies usually are affected more than lower frequencies. For this reason, *digital hearing aids*, which can be tuned to particular frequencies, are often more helpful than *analog hearing aids*, which amplify sounds at all frequencies equally.

Deaf children with severe to profound hearing losses may wear hearing aids but benefit relatively little in understanding spoken language. This does not mean that the aids are not useful, however. Hearing aids can let children know when something is happening, when someone is approaching, or when someone is speaking to them even if they cannot understand what is being said. Hearing aids also are important because they allow children to connect sounds with events in the environment, allowing them to learn about cause and effect (a falling dish breaks *and* makes a noise—that's how your mother knows it happened), about the nature of things (the intensity of her voice indicates how she feels about the broken dish), and about the nature of communication. In this last case, when mother makes a noise (e.g., through speaking) and points to a toy, the connection between things and communication gradually becomes part of the natural interactions of mother and infant. Eventually, the link between things and their names will become clear, giving words and signs meaning.

Hearing aids come in a variety of styles, models, and even colors, but they are all relatively simple devices. Regardless of whether they fit behind the ear, in the ear, or are strapped to a child's chest, hearing aids consist of a microphone, a receiver/amplifier with volume control, a miniature speaker, a battery, and an earmold (see Figure 3.1). Amplified sound picked up by the microphone passes through a tube from the receiver to the speaker to the plastic earmold custom-molded for each

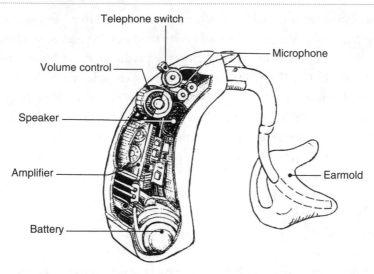

Telephone switch

Microphone

Volume control

Speaker

Amplifier

Earmold

Battery

FIGURE 3.1 Schematic drawing of a hearing aid.

user to ensure a snug fit. If you ever hear a high-pitched squeal from a child's hearing aid, it indicates that the earmold is not tightly in place, creating feedback between the microphone and a receiver.

The use of technology for improving hearing is not as simple as it might seem. Comprehension is a process that happens in the brain, not in the ear. The listener has to have enough information from the ear (and eyes) to analyze several different kinds of information in order to understand what is said. If a deaf child does not understand English speech, for example, hearing aids will help his understanding to the same extent as speaking louder to someone who does not speak English: not at all. For children with partial (or *residual*) hearing, however, the use of hearing aids can be very important. Not only do they provide them with access to the language of their (usually) hearing parents and siblings, but in cases of progressive hearing loss, they can provide a temporary bridge that will allow those children to more easily acquire sign language and reading skills with the help of spoken language. Even if they do not appear to be helping children perceive sounds, hearing aids also can be important for later cochlear implantation, stimulating the auditory nerve and keeping it healthy.

Hearing aids must be approached cautiously with very young children, however, because too much amplification can damage the young ear, perhaps speeding up or causing more hearing loss. Hearing aids (and cochlear implants) are not going to be helpful, however, if they are not working properly. Parents should check their batteries at least daily and always make sure that their children take at least one extra set with them to school.

EVERYTHING YOU ALWAYS WANTED TO KNOW ABOUT
COCHLEAR IMPLANTS

Although cochlear implants are relatively new, there has been a lot of research on their effectiveness, although "effectiveness" may have different meanings for parents, teachers, researchers, and other professionals (not to mention children themselves). Studies have shown that implants increase awareness of sound and help most deaf children to understand some speech. Partly as a result, they also can help deaf children to read better. Cochlear implants do not, however, allow deaf children to hear as well as hearing children and thus typically do not result in language or achievement equivalent to hearing peers. Cochlear implants do not "cure" deafness; they are sophisticated hearing aids. Yet, as a result of their increasing popularity, implants are altering the face of deafness and the Deaf community (see later discussion). There are still large gaps in our knowledge about educating children with implants, but the following sections provide an overview of what we currently know, holding technical details to a minimum (see Suggestions for Further Reading at the back of this book for more information).

How Implants Work

A cochlear implant has two primary parts, one that is implanted in the head and one worn outside, connected by a magnet (there are no wires poking through the scalp!). The external part of the implant is much like a hearing aid, including a microphone and a receiver that can be worn behind the ear or attached to clothing. This includes a microprocessor, which generates electrical signals of different frequencies, corresponding to sounds that vary in pitch and loudness. A wire attaches the unit to the small transmitter and the magnet. The internal part of the implant includes a small receiver and a smooth wire containing areas (electrodes) that transmit electrical impulses (see Figure 3.2). Fortunately, technological advances in cochlear implants primarily involve the software of the microprocessor, so "upgrades" do not involve additional surgery.

   Implant surgery involves making an opening above and behind the ear and hollowing a small indentation in the skull. The internal receiver fits into the indentation, and the electrode wire is threaded into the spiral of the cochlea. When activated by sounds picked up by the microphone and analyzed by the processor, the system sends signals through the transmitter, across to the receiver, and into the electrode array. The electrodes send electrical impulses to the auditory nerve at different points along the cochlea, corresponding to different sound frequencies.

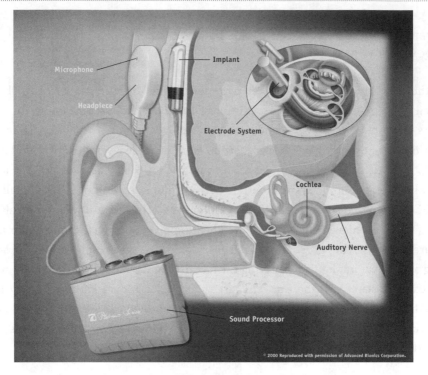

FIGURE 3.2 Schematic drawing of a cochlear implant. (Reproduced with permission of Advanced Bionics Corporation.)

About a month after implantation, when the surgical incision has healed, it is time for the initial *mapping* of the implant, where it is "tuned" to the particular hearing profile of the child. Over a series of visits to an *audiologist* (someone who specializes in hearing and amplification), the tuning will become more precise. The younger the child, typically more visits are necessary to establish optimal programming, and because responses change over time, long-term follow-up visits are required. The skill of the audiologist in programming the speech processor thus has a major impact on a child's eventual success in developing speech perception and production skills. If a child is not making progress with mapping done by her initial audiologist, it is definitely worth "getting a second opinion" somewhere else.

Once it is adjusted, the implant will offer different software programs for speech, for music, for television, and so on. All of this mapping takes time and effort, however, and it should not be assumed that a child will gain full benefit from the implant in the first weeks or even months after surgery. Reception and production of language, for example, continue to improve over at least several years in children who receive implants. This contrasts with late-deafened adults who usually obtain maximum benefit relatively quickly.

> *Asking a child to make sense of, and be able to reproduce, spoken language received only through a cochlear implant is somewhat like asking the child to recognize and draw a picture of an exotic animal they have never seen before that is standing behind a tall picket fence. Only parts of the strange animal are visible through the spaces between the wooden slats of the fence. The child must complete the image in his or her mind, imagining the shape of the parts of the animal that are not directly visible.*
>
> ---
>
> (From Spencer, P. [March, 2001.] Language performance of children with early cochlear implantation: Child and family factors. 8th Symposium on Cochlear Implants in Children. Los Angeles, CA)

Finally, it is worth noting that because of the way that the electrode wire is inserted and wound into the cochlea, residual hearing in the ear typically is lost. For this reason, cochlear implants are typically implanted in the ear with less hearing, and if complications force their removal, a hearing aid may not be effective. Contrary to some stories, however, the internal portion of an implant does not create any difficulty for swimming or sports. The child can just pull off the external portion of the implant and put it away, although just as when the batteries die, the child is then quite deaf.

The Benefits of Cochlear Implants

Just a reminder: Cochlear implants do not change deaf children into hearing children. People who have lost their hearing as adults and children who become deaf after having developed a spoken language (*postlingually*) have to learn to associate this new input with their memories of spoken language. Children who are born deaf or become deaf before spoken language is well established (*prelingually*) have a very different task in learning to understand what they receive from a cochlear implant. They have to develop language based on much more limited sound information than that received by hearing children. Furthermore, most deaf children already have delays in spoken language development before obtaining their implant, so they usually have even more difficulty in understanding whatever sound they do receive. This means that as with other hard-of-hearing children, it is important that they sit in the front of the classroom where they can always see the teacher's face. Teachers need to regularly check children's implants to be sure that the batteries are fully charged (implants use up batteries faster than hearing aids). They also need to monitor classroom discussions so that, whenever possible, there are not multiple students talking at one time. At the same time, parents and teachers need

IMPORTANT FACTORS AFFECTING SUCCESS WITH COCHLEAR IMPLANTS

- Length of time since implantation (shorter is better)
- Age at implantation (younger is better)
- Number of implants (two are better than one, especially if received at the same time)
- Degree of hearing loss (both in the implanted ear and the other ear)
- Age at hearing loss onset (older is better)
- Amount of language when hearing was lost (more is better)
- Children's cognitive abilities
- The amount and types of postimplantation therapy received.

to ensure that the emphasis on speech and hearing when a child receives an implant does not lead them to overlook the child's need to develop greater visual skills (see Chapter 6).

It is important to recognize that there are large individual differences among children in how well they do with cochlear implants. Several factors have been shown to benefit their speech, language, and academic outcomes. Even when we are able to sort out the contributions of these different factors, we still are faced with the fact that we do not know whether there is some minimum or ideal amount of exposure to spoken language necessary after cochlear implantation. Cochlear implants are designed to facilitate speech and hearing, and it should not be surprising that they often lead to better spoken language skills than would be the case (for the same children) without implants. There is no evidence, however, that sign language interferes with the development of spoken language—for children with or without cochlear implants (see Chapter 4).

We mentioned earlier that because cochlear implants generally give deaf children better access to sound, including spoken language, they can lead to better academic achievement. Research has demonstrated that earlier cochlear implantation leads to better hearing, speech, and language and, presumably as a result, somewhat better reading skills. Implantation after 2 years of age now is considered "late," where just a decade ago "late" referred to implantation after 10 or 11 years of age. All of this means that most children receiving cochlear implants today have them as they are acquiring language, and thus they most grow up with spoken language as their first language. Importantly, however, because children gain differing amounts of hearing after implantation, they vary widely in how much speech they achieve and the extent to which their hearing and language gains influence reading and other areas of academic achievement. Of particular concern are some recent findings indicating that although elementary school deaf children may show significant benefits to reading from cochlear implantation, those benefits become smaller by the time they reach high school. This is not to say that the cochlear implant becomes less effective. Rather, it appears that we have not yet learned how best to educate children with cochlear implants. When they are in regular school classrooms, they usually are treated as though they are hearing students; when they are in schools or programs for the deaf, they usually are treated as though they are deaf students. Audiologically and perhaps cognitively (see Chapters 6–8), they really are neither, even when they have good spoken language.

Recent studies have suggested that children who have received cochlear implants—and thus depend primarily on spoken language—also can benefit from using a signed language during the school years. In fact, we are only aware of one study in which students with cochlear implants showed academic achievement fully equivalent to hearing peers, and that involved students with implants who also had received classroom support from sign language interpreters throughout the school years. Some implant surgeons, audiologists, and speech-language therapists nevertheless continue to warn parents away from sign language in the belief that it will interfere with a child's acquisition of spoken language. Other cochlear implant centers are more supportive of deaf children's signing, believing that "more language is better," regardless of whether the language is visual or auditory.

Because cochlear implantation is aimed at improving a child's hearing and speech, we understand the need for intensive hearing and speech practice with those children. Yet the primary basis for the anti–sign language position for children with cochlear implants is the assumption that because sign language is so much easier to learn than spoken language, deaf children will become "lazy" and sign rather than speak. If sign language is that much easier for children to acquire, that should tell us something. Clearly, there needs to be research aimed at objectively evaluating how, when, and why sign language and spoken language influence each other and what combination best serves the needs of deaf children in educational and other settings. Presently, however, many supporters of cochlear implantation for children remain opposed to sign language, and many supporters of early sign language remain opposed to cochlear implants. In this climate, such research is unlikely to occur, with deaf children most likely being the biggest losers. Let us therefore consider these issues more closely.

The Politics of Cochlear Implants

Anyone who has looked into cochlear implants, especially for children, likely has discovered the related controversies. We have already touched on the belief of many that spoken language is so difficult for deaf children to acquire—even with cochlear implants—that all of their energies need to be directed to speech and hearing. Indeed, we have heard of parents having to sign documents promising not to allow their child to learn a signed language if they are to receive an implant. On the other side of the debate, some Deaf people believe that "forcing cochlear implants on children" does not allow them the opportunity to develop normal identities and freedom of choice. Having a cochlear implant, in their view, communicates to the child that being deaf is bad; and that this message may leave the child forever caught between Deaf and hearing cultures and a member of neither.

Research thus far suggests that fears about difficulties in deaf children's social-emotional development with cochlear implants are unfounded. Although it is unclear how well children with implants become integrated into the hearing community—largely determined by just how good their hearing and speech become—implants do not appear to create any greater social or emotional difficulties for deaf children than do hearing aids. There are now so many children with cochlear implants and organizations aimed at supporting them and their families that a deaf child with an implant often will find a peer group of other children with implants.

Several studies that have looked at their social integration with hearing children have reported parents' claims that their implanted children have hearing friends and interact with hearing peers in a variety of settings. Little information is available, however, on deaf children's view of the situation, and what evidence is available suggests that they may not always be as comfortable with hearing peers as their parents believe. In part, this may reflect pressures to justify the cost of a cochlear implant and the extensive, long-term therapy associated with it. Alternatively, it may be that parents only see their children at home and may not fully appreciate how their child functions in a peer group. As with hearing, speech, and language, the one certainty is that children with cochlear implants vary widely in their social-emotional functioning in various settings. Some see themselves as hearing, some see themselves as deaf, and many others see themselves, as one young girl reported, "not quite deaf and not quite hearing." As in other areas, it therefore is important to treat these children as individuals and not make decisions based on the kinds of hearing technology they use.

Unfortunately, hearing parents are often bombarded with one-sided arguments from advocates and opponents of implants that make objective decision making difficult. Many parents, for example, report being told at the time of their newborn's hearing screening that cochlear implantation is absolutely necessary if deaf children are ever to be able to acquire language and be educated in school. Once again, the research suggests that this all-or-none view of implants, language, and learning is wrong—but don't blame your audiologist for this! Many people in the speech and hearing field are relatively unfamiliar with people who are comfortable and content with being deaf/Deaf. They primarily meet people who are unhappy or traumatized by hearing loss and therefore desire change. Efforts to decrease the emotion and increase objectivity in the discussion of cochlear implants for children seem to be working. Nonetheless, the debate continues, and parents have to try to ignore the propaganda that often surrounds this issue.

FINAL WORDS

It is through hearing that most children acquire the native language of their society. We understand the challenges faced by parents and teachers when children do not share their language. Yet exposing a deaf child only to spoken language—the way one might try to "immerse" a child from another country in a new language— usually does not work very well. Hearing aids, cochlear implants, and other technologies help children gain access to sounds in their environment, including speech. None of them provide access equal to that of normal hearing, however, and that is one reason why we say that deaf children are not hearing children who cannot hear. Similarly, sign language, print, and other forms of visual communication offer deaf children windows onto the world and avenues for learning, but they too have different requirements and outcomes than the spoken language that surrounds a hearing child. These are not situations of *better* or *worse*, but of *different*.

Teachers of many deaf and hard-of-hearing children will quickly recognize that their students may have somewhat less content knowledge than hearing peers in some areas, likely due to less than full access to language and learning previously. Deaf children's and hard-of-hearing children's difficulties in reading and writing are both a cause and an effect of that situation (see Chapter 8). At the same time, teachers also will see that those students have all of the necessary intellectual tools to learn and thrive in the classroom. There will be differences in how they learn because of differences in what they know, how they use that knowledge, and the particular skills they bring with them, but none of these need stand in the way of academic success. Later chapters describe some of these differences in how they can be accommodated in the classroom and in informal learning situations. In the meantime, we turn to the ways in which the foundations of learning are established through communication, language, and social interaction.

4

LANGUAGE AND COMMUNICATION

IT MAY SEEM that throughout this book we are obsessed with language. Okay, we are—but with good reason. It should be apparent by this point that the acquisition of language is a critical component of normal development for both deaf and hearing children. Early language fluency is important both in its own right and as it supports social development, cognitive development, and further language development. Although it sometimes appears that children achieve language quite naturally and easily, it frequently involves explicit instruction at home and in the classroom. As we described earlier, the vast majority of children's knowledge and experience comes in the form of language or is accompanied by language. Thus, our perceptions and conceptions of the world are often colored as much by the way something is described as by its reality (see the discussion of Crustaceans in Chapter 2).

This is not a language development book, and we will not describe the processes and products of language acquisition in any detail. If you have an interest in this area, we encourage you to pick up a language development textbook for descriptions of the complexities and far-reaching interrelations of language and other aspects of development. In the sections that follow, we will focus on language as it both supports and is supported by deaf children's educational experiences, primarily during the school years.

UNDERSTANDING LANGUAGE

For all of its importance, language acquisition is a considerable challenge for the vast majority of deaf children, and most have parents and teachers who are not entirely sure how best to help them (see Box 4.1). Deaf children of deaf parents have the benefit of full access to language from birth through a natural visual

---

BOX 4.1

SOME COMMON MYTHS ABOUT DEAF CHILDREN'S LANGUAGE
(EACH FOLLOWED BY WHAT WE REALLY KNOW FROM RESEARCH)

- *Signed languages are an inferior form of communication primarily useful for "oral failures."* Natural sign languages fully support child development and education. American Sign Language, spoken English, French Sign Language, and spoken French, for example, are all true languages and none is inferior to another.

- *Learning to sign interferes with learning to speak.* This myth has long been passed from professional to professional, but there is no evidence to support it. Sometimes learning to sign actually facilitates acquisition of spoken language by deaf children and other times it is independent of it.

- *Any deaf child can learn to speak.* Perhaps, but not necessarily with sufficient intelligibility for people outside of the family to understand him. Programs that advertise this claim do not accept (or eventually transfer out) deaf children who do not have or do not acquire sufficient spoken language skills.

- *Identification and intervention within the first 6 months enables deaf children to develop language normally.* Even with early identification and intervention, deaf children typically fall in the bottom 25% of the range of "normal" language development compared to hearing peers.

- *Deaf children with cochlear implants develop normal speech and language.* Many of them develop better speech and language, but rarely as good as hearing children. These children receive extensive speech training, which also contributes to the speech intelligibility; it is not the implant alone.

- *Children with cochlear implants should not be allowed to learn sign language.* There is no evidence that this is harmful, and there is even some evidence that it leads to better academic and social outcomes.

- *Hard-of-hearing children develop language and academic skills similar to hearing children.* Those children often have good speech, leading to the assumption that they hear better than they really do. In fact, even children with minimal hearing losses frequently demonstrate language and academic delays.

- *Deaf children's language delays simply are due to their lack of hearing.* Blind children show many of the same spoken language delays as deaf children, indicating that there is more to language acquisition than just hearing a language.

language, and the work of several researchers has indicated that those children pass various milestones of language development in the same order and at the same rate as hearing children if not faster, at least early on. Nevertheless, there still may be challenges. For one thing, they are likely to be exposed to fewer fluent language users than hearing children of the same age, and they will miss many of the opportunities for incidental language learning that hearing children have by virtue of overhearing the conversations of others (where else would they learn those bad words?) and watching television and movies. It also may be important that about 95% of their parents had hearing parents, and thus they are not true native users of sign language themselves.

The extent to which coming from a multigeneration deaf family makes for differences in language development has not yet been explored, but deaf children of deaf parents have been reported to have somewhat better reading abilities than deaf children with hearing parents. The actual finding is that better sign language skills are associated with better reading abilities. But better spoken language skills also are associated with better reading abilities. The important factor therefore is not that the parents are deaf or their use of sign language. Rather, because they are able to provide their children with earlier and more fluent access to language than most hearing parents, deaf parents are able to offer their deaf children greater support for literacy (reading and writing) and cognitive development as well as for language development. Better early reading skills also should support language development, exposing those children to wider vocabularies and greater knowledge of the world that, in turn, will support further learning (see Figure 2.1 in Chapter 2).

If the deaf parents of a deaf child had hearing parents themselves, that means their own early vocabularies were acquired from (hearing) parents who may not have been able to communicate fluently with them and thus might have been delayed or incomplete. Those deaf parents might have passed along to their own children delays in language or in particular areas of language development. Young deaf children, for example, often are less likely to spontaneously use existing vocabulary in learning new words/signs (see Box 4.2). That strategy may need to be explicitly taught to deaf children, even if young hearing children bring it into the learning environment already well formed.

Findings like these emphasize that while we frequently take language development for granted, it really is a complex and demanding problem-solving task. Most obvious, perhaps, are the many ways in which early social interactions and other experiences depend upon interpersonal communication and help to support the continuing development of language. We will consider this issue in the next chapter, highlighting the contributions of early interactions to learning and to education.

BOX 4.2
LEARNING NEW WORDS USING OLD WORDS

Readers who have taken a course in language development or have children of their own will be familiar with the *vocabulary burst* or *vocabulary spurt* that occurs about 18 months of age, when hearing children appear to be acquiring up to 10 to 20 new words a day. Clearly, all of those words are not being taught to the child, but they are learned using other words. For example, suppose a child is shown a picture containing a horse, a bird, and a shark—and that "horse" and "bird" are already in her vocabulary. If she is asked to point to the shark and can do so, it shows that she realizes that "shark" must name the only one of the three animals she does not know. This kind of word learning begins at about 18 months in hearing children and is likely responsible for the vocabulary burst. However, this kind of word learning generally does not appear among deaf children of deaf parents until 3 to 5 years of age. We currently are studying whether this simply reflects a difference in the way that deaf children learn new vocabulary from their deaf parents or if it might be due to how those deaf parents learned vocabulary from their own hearing parents. To do this, we are looking at vocabulary learning in children of first-generation deaf parents compared to deaf parents from multigeneration deaf families. Some deaf children from multi-generation deaf families show vocabulary spurts and some do not. The reason(s) for this is not yet clear.

FROM COMMUNICATION TO LANGUAGE

The question *To sign or not to sign?* is just one of a large number of issues facing the family of a deaf child, but in some ways it is the most central one. For many parents, accepting that their child is deaf is difficult enough, and choosing a signed language as their child's first language seems like a big step. Some parents therefore first seek to have their children acquire spoken language, something that is particularly difficult for very young deaf children. Unfortunately, the relative merits of spoken language versus sign language for deaf children are frequently clouded by disagreement, personal opinions, and what appear to be contradictory research findings. We will sidestep that controversy here and focus on the importance of successful communication.

Our own reading of the history of deaf education as well as the available research on language development and educational outcomes among deaf children has led us to conclude that sign language can play an important role in the early communication mix for most young deaf children, with or without cochlear implants, and for many hard-of-hearing children as well. Most centrally, however, it must be recognized that different children will benefit from different communication alternatives, and it may be that some children will benefit most from the availability of both spoken language and sign language while others do just fine with one or the other.

Deaf children who learn to sign at a young age, with or without accompanying spoken language, have been found to do better in school during the early years and have better social relationships with their parents and peers compared to children with similar hearing levels who are raised only with spoken language. Among deaf university students, in contrast, these benefits are reduced or completely absent. Still unclear is whether the advantages of earlier sign language become less with the acquisition of other skills or if they are less important for better students— those who go on to university. In any case, there are many deaf children, most notably those with cochlear implants, who use only spoken language. In some countries, including the United Kingdom and Australia, the majority of deaf children initially are enrolled in programs focused exclusively on spoken language. Those programs are not always successful, but early intervention, digital hearing aids, and especially cochlear implants have brought us a long way from the mid-1980s, when over half of all deaf children in Canada and the United States were reported to have unintelligible speech.

It is easy enough to understand the desire of most hearing parents to have a child who speaks and hears like them. Few deaf children, however, will ever talk like their hearing brothers and sisters, and most will not be proficient at understanding the speech of others. Contrary to the popular myth, very few individuals with severe to profound hearing losses can read lips well enough for the purposes of everyday communication. Lipreading or *speechreading* is difficult, tiring, and error prone, depending as much or more on the characteristics of the speaker and the context than the skills of the deaf person. Research findings indicate that deaf adults generally understand only about 30% of what is said via speechreading alone, without additional contextual information. Thus, speechreading proficiency is not something that should be expected from young deaf children.

Some parents believe that learning to sign will interfere with the acquisition of spoken language and thus may resist the notion of their child learning a signed language for as long as possible. People who argue in favor of that position depend almost entirely on the laziness argument we described in Chapter 2. That is, because (they admit) sign language is easier for a child to learn than spoken language, the child will be lazy and not use her speech. The only research evidence we can find relevant to that argument comes from a single study indicating that young children who had both sign language and spoken language skills were more likely

to sign than to speak. The reason, however, was that they were more likely to be understood when they signed than when they spoke—not because they were lazy. Furthermore, as we have already noted, several other studies have found that that the acquisition of a signed language actually can support the learning of spoken language.

Delaying the learning of a signed language in the hope of better speaking skills in deaf children—like delaying cochlear implantation—has not been shown to have any advantages. More commonly, such delays make matters more difficult for both children and their parents. The first years of life are when basic language skills develop, and the first 2–3 years are generally recognized as a critical period for language learning. There is no substitute for natural language learning, and language acquisition that begins at age 3 or 4 is not natural.

SIGNED LANGUAGES AND VISUAL COMMUNICATION SYSTEMS

Almost every country has its own sign language. Some countries have more than one, corresponding to their multiple spoken languages. Like spoken languages, signed languages vary widely, having their own accents and dialects. Some signs may be limited to particular schools or regions (Pittsburgh, Pennsylvania, and Manchester, England, are two good examples). In any case, deaf children's exposure to a *natural sign language* is very different from exposure to *sign systems*, which are based on spoken language grammars and usually designed to help deaf children learn to read. The available research indicates that those artificial systems do not promote fluency in either the natural sign languages or the spoken languages underlying them. Furthermore, the evidence suggests they do not support reading any better than natural sign languages—the reason why they were created in the first place.

Natural Sign Languages

Like a spoken language, a natural sign language consists of a large vocabulary of signs and rules that govern how sentences are constructed and combined (*grammar*). American Sign Language (ASL) is the natural sign language used by deaf signers in the United States and most of Canada, as well as in some other countries. It is very different from British Sign Language (BSL), even though English is spoken in both the United States and Great Britain.

In most signed languages, individual signs are composed of a handshape, a place of articulation, movement, and whether one or two hands are used. Changes in one of these elements can change the meaning of a sign if the result is a real sign, just like changing a letter in a word ("read," "bead," and "lead" versus "gead"). Signs also can be modified just as words can be changed by adding certain beginnings or endings ("dog" becomes "dogs," "complain" becomes "complaining," etc.). In addition, signs can be modified by *nonmanual markers* such as the raising or lowering of the eyebrows, indicating different kinds of questions. Signed languages also have *classifiers*, particular handshapes that have general-purpose or categorical meanings. In ASL, for example, an upright 1-hand (a raised index finger) may be used for representing an individual (human), and a 3-hand (made with the thumb up and the first two fingers pointing away from the signer) may be used to represent CAR or other vehicles. Other types of classifiers function as adjectives, indicating the size, shape, or location of objects. Spoken English does not use classifiers, but some spoken languages, like Navajo, Thai, and Japanese, do.

Together with signs, facial expression, and body movement, signed languages also make use of manual alphabets. When referring to a concept that does not have a sign, or when a sign is unknown, signers often use *fingerspelling* to "spell out" words. Different sign languages use different manual alphabets. In British Sign Language and Turkish Sign Language, for example, two hands are used to represent the letters of the alphabet (although in different ways), whereas in ASL only one hand is used. Some signed languages, like Hong Kong Sign Language, do not use fingerspelling at all.[1] Deaf children often comprehend fingerspelled words before they can read, because they perceive the handshapes and movements as signs rather than as strings of individual letters comprising a word. As they get older and learn to read, they come to recognize that fingerspelled words are made up of letters and, in a sense, must learn to fingerspell all over again.

Where Do Signed Languages Come from?

Contrary to frequent assumptions, "sign language" is not an international gesture system. Different sign languages emerged in different geographical regions, just as spoken languages did. Also like spoken languages, some current sign languages emerged from earlier languages. ASL, for example, came about through a combination of the grammar of French Sign Language (LSF) and American signs brought from England and France as well as others borrowed from Native Americans (who generally used them in dealings between tribes, not for everyday within-tribe communication).

All "living" languages, languages currently being used by communities, evolve through both natural and artificial mechanisms. Because signed languages are relatively young, there have been efforts to standardize signs within some sign languages, particularly rarely used but educationally important signs such as those used in science and mathematics. In New Zealand, for example, deaf and hearing linguists and educators collaborated on the standardization of mathematical signs to be used in schools and they are now becoming part of New Zealand Sign Language (NZSL).

In contrast to the New Zealand approach, several groups in the United States have created sign dictionaries, now collected and sometimes allowing user input through the Internet. Unfortunately, various educators, technologists, interpreters, and linguists have created sites for their own purposes with differing standards, rules, and opportunities for sharing. These sites are useful for discovery of sign alternatives, but the lack of collaboration means that standardization and use in education are a long way off.

Teachers who are skilled signers have other ways to communicate concepts that do not have established signs. Science teachers often use animation, figures, and photos as a part of their teaching, and many would find it difficult to teach without these aids. Science teachers who sign also can offer students the benefit of watching an "animation" using signs, gestures, and space. For example, clearly describing mitosis (the process of cell division) is much easier in sign language than in spoken language, using depiction and classifiers with signed explanation. Such communication strategies frequently are found among skilled signers but less often among late learners who tend to sign word for word while thinking in spoken language. Those people, however, are not really using *sign language*, but some hybrid form of manual communication.

Sign and Visual Communication Systems

Over the past few generations, educators have come to realize that the use of hearing aids and cochlear implants to aid deaf students' hearing often is not enough for them to attain language fluency. As a result, educators and others have developed systems to show spoken language on the hands. As hybrids rather than true languages, their implications for language development, cognitive development, and literacy are still not entirely clear.

Signed English

Among the more complex systems constructed by educators to help deaf children learn to understand English is *Signed English*, which combines some ASL signs, English word order, and grammatical markers (plurals, *-ing*, etc.).[2] *Seeing Essential English*, or *SEE1*, and *Signing Exact English*, or *SEE2*, similarly were developed as ways to represent English visually on the hands, although they have different rules. In SEE1, every English word has a basic sign, and signs are produced in English word order. Additional signs are used to represent English grammatical structures, as in Signed English. SEE2 goes further, using a different sign for each *morpheme* (meaningful unit) of English rather than for each concept. So, where ASL and Signed English have single signs for concepts like *butterfly* and *sweetheart*, SEE2 uses two signs, one for each part of the compound word. *Butterfly* is signed by combining the signs BUTTER and FLY, and *sweetheart* is signed by combining the signs SWEET and HEART. Both of these examples seem conceptually misleading, but they may be no more so than the English compound words.

Another common feature of signed English systems is that they frequently "initialize" the beginning of signs. For example, the generic sign for a group of people can be initialized with a C handshape for "class" or an A handshape for "association." There are also groups of signs made with different letter handshapes to give it several different but related meanings, for example HAVE ending with V ("have"), S ("has"), or D ("had"). Skilled deaf and hearing signers sometimes use initialized signs even if new signers are taught that they are not really part of ASL.

Simultaneous Communication

The use of variations of Signed English by teachers and parents is usually due to their not having fluency in a natural sign language, so they rely on their primary language to help express themselves visually. Some teachers who are fluent signers nonetheless use signed forms of English at times to teach new vocabulary, support reading, or demonstrate relationships between sign language and spoken language.

For children who have some hearing, the teacher might speak and sign at the same time, what is referred to in the United States as *simultaneous communication* or *SimCom* and in other countries as *sign-supported speech*. Studies of hearing children of deaf parents and of communities with a large number of deaf members indicate that hearing native signers do not naturally use simultaneous communication. Instead, they switch from one language to another depending on the situation.

Some teachers are excellent simultaneous communication users (and usually are excellent signers as well), fully capturing English while utilizing characteristics of ASL such as the use of space, pointing, and so on. Research has shown that in the hands of a good simultaneous communicator, high school and college students learn just as much as they do from teachers using ASL, but similar studies apparently have not been done with younger students. The problem for less skilled signers is that simultaneous communication makes it harder for them to monitor their own signing. They hear their speech and do not detect their errors in the signs, facial expressions, and body movements that are part of true signed languages. This reduces the comprehensibility of their signing while hindering further development of their sign language skills.

Simultaneous communication potentially could have advantages for children with cochlear implants or hearing aids, helping them to catch words or signs that they missed or did not understand. Like Signed English, however, it has a bad reputation from both linguistic and cultural perspectives. Nevertheless, there are more people using simultaneous communication with deaf students inside and outside of school than people who communicate in a true signed language, and it therefore seems a topic worthy of further investigation.

Language Cueing Systems

One alternative to signing is the use of *cued speech*. Cued speech is a supplement to spoken language intended to make it fully visible. It has been estimated that only about 20%–30% of spoken English is visible on the lips, for example, and many speech sounds look alike when they are pronounced. For example, pronunciation of the letters "m," "p," and "b" all look the same, making it impossible to speechread the words "mat," "pat," and "bat" without context. "Card" and "guard" look the same because the /k/ sound and the /g/ sound are hidden inside the mouth.

Cued English uses eight handshapes and four locations in addition to mouth movements to represent English *phonemes* or speech sounds. Cues for vowel sounds are produced by placing the hand at one of the four locations from the chest to the head, while consonants are cued by making one of eight handshapes in a vowel location. Through cueing, "mat," "pat," and "bat" are distinguishable because the initial consonants have different handshapes, helping deaf children recognize which sounds are being used. The handshapes of cued speech thus play a very different role from the handshapes of signed languages, which carry information about meaning rather than about sound. Cued speech has been found to support literacy skills among deaf children learning regular languages like French and Spanish, but there does not appear to be any evidence that it helps children to read English.

Some programs use cued speech to *teach* speech. That is not the purpose of the system, which, like other systems, was developed to support literacy. Cued speech transliterators (like interpreters) therefore do not use their voices when they cue, and some speak for deaf students who cue without using voice. Even though it is called cued *speech*, it really is a system to supplement speechreading, not hearing. One problem with cued speech that also occurs with sign language is that hearing adults and other language models often use it only when talking directly to a deaf child but not when talking among themselves. This deprives the deaf child of opportunities to learn how other individuals talk to each other and learn from what they say. Hearing cuers also often know how to cue better than they know how to read cues, so deaf cuers are expected to speak to hearing adults. Using different codes for comprehension and production can create cognitive challenges both inside and outside of the classroom.

Visual Phonics is a system that appears similar to the cued speech system, but it isn't. Visual Phonics is aimed at helping children to understand that speech sounds are the building blocks of language and develop the ability to use and manipulate them. Like cued speech, Visual Phonics uses a system of hand signals produced together with spoken language in order to make visible features of articulation that cannot be distinguished through speechreading, but it differs from cued speech in other ways. For example, while cued speech is used to support spoken language, Visual Phonics is used in the classroom specifically to teach phonics in support of reading. Cued speech also provides information about sounds themselves but not how they are produced. The handshapes of Visual Phonics, in contrast, incorporate visual elements that remind students of the articulatory movements necessary to produce the sounds.

Several researchers have suggested that Visual Phonics might support *phonological development* (the understanding of speech sounds) for deaf and hard-of-hearing children, regardless of whether they depend primarily on sign or spoken language. Preliminary studies support that prediction, because both deaf and hard-of-hearing children have been shown to increase their skills in word reading, decoding of new words, and reading comprehension, but more studies are needed.

SPOKEN COMMUNICATION

Up to now, this chapter has included relatively little discussion of spoken language. The primary reason for this is that the focus here is on deaf children with greater hearing losses, those who are less likely to benefit from exposure to spoken language unless they also benefit from cochlear implants or hearing aids. The claim is not that other deaf children cannot learn to speak; surely some of them can. Rather, the point is that in the absence of hearing (especially during the critical stages of language learning), spoken communication is rarely viable as the primary means of communication for deaf children. With extensive speech training, many deaf children reach the point where family members can understand their speech, but that does not mean that they will be understood by others outside the family or that they will be able to understand the speech of others.

We have all seen deaf people on television or elsewhere who appear to have excellent or at least pretty good speech. In many cases, those are individuals with lesser hearing losses or people who had better hearing when they learned to speak and then experienced progressive or acute hearing losses. Others have improved their speech as older children or as adults. Often, this shift occurs after using sign language early in life, at the point where an individual has the motivation and ability to benefit from spoken language methods. And still, there are exceptions like several of our deaf (and Deaf) colleagues and Heather Whitestone, Miss America 1994, who were raised with intensive speech therapy and have very good speech. There are several schools and programs in this country offering education exclusively in spoken language and claiming varying degrees of success.[3] Still to be determined is whether the children who succeed in such programs are representative of all deaf children or whether they have particular characteristics that make them most likely to benefit from such exposure in the first place. In any case, the argument for exclusive exposure to spoken language has never been supported in any broad sense and thus, for the present, spoken language seems most likely to be effective when combined with a signed language or some alternative.

Learning to Speak

Speech training and speech assessment should be thought of as a whole, not as two different endeavors. Assessment of a child's skills and needs is essential to effective teaching of spoken language, and the progress of teaching requires regular assessments both of progress in speech skill acquisition and possible changes in young children's hearing. Both assessment and training therefore have to take into consideration the goals and capabilities of the children and their families, and not just some vague notion about the importance of spoken language. Indeed, it is the intense adherence to the primacy of speech by some advocates of "oral app-roaches" to education that drives many deaf individuals away from its potential benefits.

The goal of speech and speechreading training should be to allow deaf children to take advantage of the most information possible and have access to the full range of opportunities offered to hearing children. As we will see, speech training can take on a variety of forms, depending on the needs of the individual child. Different programs focus on different levels of spoken language, from individual letter sounds, through syllables, to whole-word pronunciation methods. Syllable methods, for example, involve repeated practice with single consonant-vowel pairs such as *pa, pu, pa* or sets of pairs that vary in their vowel "place of articulation" such as the set that would sound like *pee, pa, peh, po, pu*, where you can feel the tongue moving farther and farther back in the mouth. Examples like this are not visible on the mouth (look in the mirror again) and are extremely difficult for deaf children to learn; hence the potential usefulness of cued speech. Alternatively, speech training can focus on the pronunciation of whole words. This is often done with words in isolation, although their presentation within meaningful contexts can also contribute to reading as well as speechreading skill. Finally, what was long called the "natural method" of teaching speech to deaf children emphasizes its use in natural situations, with less reliance on practice drills.

Regardless of its level, speech training usually involves one-on-one interaction with a trained speech therapist who models articulation and gives feedback on speech over many sessions. Parents are given exercises to work on at home with their child, but this is rarely sufficient for fluent speech production. There are also a variety of technological tools available for professional and home use for speech training. For example, there is interactive computer software in which young chil-dren's productions of correct sounds lead to interesting visual events, such as a monkey climbing a tree. Older children might be shown speech patterns on the computer screen and work to match them with their own productions. These and other methods serve to help coordinate motor movements of the tongue and mouth and appropriate inflow and outflow of air as well as helping the child to become more comfortable with speech training.

To be most effective, speech training must be coupled with appropriate amplifi-cation, so that children can receive auditory feedback in addition to what they can see on the lips. If they have sufficient residual (aided) hearing and speechreading skills to also comprehend the spoken language of others, spoken language can be a valuable tool. There are several different approaches to enhancing spoken language by deaf children, however, and the apparent disagreements among their advocates are just as bewildering as are those among advocates of different sign systems (with perhaps even less support for any particular system).

Oral Methods

There are various methods intended to give deaf and hard-of-hearing children knowledge of and the ability to produce sounds and structures of a given language. Perhaps the most common and obvious of these is simple lipreading, or *speechreading*, but we have already seen that this is far more difficult and less helpful than is generally supposed. Other methods are more complex and, of course, each has its supporters. In general, however, formal approaches to teaching deaf children spoken language all include four characteristics deemed essential to their success:

- Beginning therapy as early as possible after identification of hearing loss
- Early fitting of hearing aids, their consistent use, and careful supervision to ensure that they are in working order and used properly
- Active involvement of parents and siblings to ensure consistent spoken language models and support for language use
- Encouraging the child to participate—using spoken language—in a variety of activities inside and outside of school.

Let us consider the two primary approaches, at least in North America, the *auditory verbal* and the *auditory oral* methods.

Auditory Verbal Therapy

Auditory verbal therapy (AVT) is best known for its focus on enhancing deaf children's listening skills and limiting the use of speechreading. During therapy sessions, the therapist's mouth is usually covered, so that children cannot make use of visual cues to comprehension (clearly this method requires that the child have some amount of hearing). Proponents of AVT emphasize the importance of mainstream education but couple it with intensive one-on-one speech therapy, especially for younger children. Regardless of whether children are using hearing aids or have cochlear implants, parents are trained to carefully monitor the equipment (it is amazing how often teachers find children coming to school with dead batteries in their hearing aids and implants) to ensure that their child maximizes use of their residual hearing. Therapists are seen as supporting parents, who are given the primary responsibility for their child's success.

Most centrally, the emphasis of AVT is on children's use of spoken language in a variety of social and family settings, and it is intended to result in hearing becoming a central part of the child's personality. Sound and speech are supposed to become rewarding, so that the child is motivated to utilize her residual hearing and speech skills.

The Auditory Oral Method

The auditory oral (AO) approach to spoken language development is similar to AVT, with some different emphases. The primary differences between the two methods relate to their relative emphasis on audition and vision and differences in the kinds and location of therapy. Most prominently, the AO method allows children to make use of speechreading as well as residual hearing to support both comprehension and production of spoken language. The emphasis of most AO practitioners on the use of visual cues has been diminished, and while they still allow children to make use of speechreading and gesture, many no longer encourage their use.

AVT and the AO approache also differ with regard to their philosophies concerning educational placement for deaf children. Unlike the AVT emphasis on mainstream school placements, the AO approach includes supporting children in a variety of settings, from separate classrooms for deaf and hard-of-hearing children to reverse mainstream to full or partial mainstreaming in a regular classroom. Students also may move from one kind of program to another, depending on their needs and preferences, throughout the school years. Finally, whereas AVT emphasizes the "natural method," AO therapy often includes more drill and practice.

FINAL WORDS

Given the several alternative communication systems available for deaf children, it might seem that combining as many sources of information as possible (although not necessarily at the same time) is a good idea. That was the philosophy behind *total communication*, which advocated the use of sign, speech, and support for hearing through assistive listening devices as they best suited each individual child. At present, however, it remains unclear whether any of the various combinations of signs/cues and spoken language benefit deaf children's achievement or spoken language skills enough to offset their not being fluent in either a signed or a spoken language. For the most part, combined systems were developed to provide a bridge from sign language to print literacy, but the theoretical case is much stronger than the evidence of their success.

Learning sign language (or learning a very different spoken language for that matter) admittedly is not easy for hearing adults. It also is difficult for hearing parents to find skilled signers for their deaf children to interact with, and it is not easy to find time for adult sign classes. But deaf children are able to learn signed vocabulary and language naturally, just as they do spoken language, as long as they are exposed to enough fluent users of the language. Although long-term educational implications of fluency in sign language and/or spoken language are still unclear, at least by college age, deaf students who use diverse communication systems such as cued speech, ASL, and Signed English do equally well in the classroom. Whether this is a reflection of the resilience of deaf children or the possibility that only those who are able to overcome communication barriers make it to the college level remains to be determined.

There is a joke in Europe: "What do you call a person who knows only one language?" The answer: "an American." Most people on earth know more than one language. In the United States, however, knowing more than one language is often not appreciated by those who believe that English is the only language that matters. We are not denying that English is important, but we are suggesting that for many deaf children neither English nor sign language will be sufficient. Deaf students at all levels seem to be better off academically and socially if they are bilingual rather than monolingual. There are well-documented benefits to learning a signed language and no evidence of negative consequences. As researchers and educators, we believe that adding a natural sign language to the environment will have a positive impact on most deaf children's cognitive, language, social, and educational development regardless of their hearing levels.

5

FAMILY AND PEERS

Foundations of Learning

CHAPTER 2 INTRODUCED the idea that language, learning, and experience all affect each other in a child's development (see Figure 2.1). The point was to emphasize that children do not grow up in a vacuum, and that what is considered "normal" varies widely because children are constantly influenced by people, events, and the environment around them. Everything they learn changes who they are and therefore affects later behavior and learning. Sometimes this *cumulative* quality of development (building the new on what is already there) is obvious, for example, when a child's learning to count changes the way he moves a game piece when playing a board game. At other times, the influence of prior learning is much more subtle, and parents may not notice when their child first recognizes that three dots on a page represent the same number, regardless of whether they form a line, an obvious triangle, or a seemingly random pattern.

A lot of what a young child knows—like "three is three"—comes simply from play and interacting with the world. Other knowledge comes from mental experimentation: thinking about things, understanding relations or the way things work, and sometimes trying them out in the real world. Probably the majority of a child's knowledge at any given time, however, comes from other people who provide new information, new behaviors, and new things with which to interact. In this sense, the family and peers are major contributors to development and learning.

EDUCATION BEGINS AT HOME

Parents and siblings (and even the family dog) provide infants and toddlers with the earliest interactions that support learning in social, language, and cognitive areas. Because at least 95% of deaf children are born to nonsigning, hearing parents, early communication usually is not a simple matter. Regardless of whether or not they have hearing aids or cochlear implants and whether they primarily use sign language or spoken language, it is through vision and touch that deaf infants will gain access to the world of experience.

During the first months of life, mothers and infants develop ways of interacting with each other through a variety of shared experiences, from diaper changing to "dancing" around in the nursery. Eventually, their actions become intertwined in a way that teaches children simple routines, provides information about successful and unsuccessful social interactions, and begins the *cumulative* learning process (Figure 2.1). Those actions also contribute to the emotional bonding between parents and children. Is anything different when the child is deaf?

Well, for the most part, it's the same. But not always. When a hearing baby fusses, she is likely to stop crying (at least temporarily) when she hears mother approach. A deaf infant, in contrast, will not hear mother approach and soothing words will have little or no impact. Some parents feel anxious or rejected by the lack of social responses from their deaf baby, but it's nothing personal! Over time, hearing mothers of deaf babies—just like deaf mothers with hearing or deaf babies—rely more and more on vision and touch, discovering that physical contact can be soothing for both baby and parent. (It may be helpful to hum while holding the baby close, so she can feel the vibrations.) Waving, smiling, and exaggerated facial expressions soon will bring waving and smiling in return. In addition to helping to establish emotional bonds between parents and children, these early nonvocal interactions teach about turn-taking, cause-effect, and social behavior.

Deaf parents have a variety of visual and tactile (touch) strategies for interacting with their young children. When we see these behaviors, they look natural, but discovering and using them consistently can be a real challenge for hearing parents. Consider the examples in Box 5.1. Not only do these help to get and maintain the attention of deaf children, they implicitly teach children strategies they can use themselves in interactions with family members and peers. Over time, these strategies become more flexible, and parents (and children) learn to modify them to fit different situations. Whether at home or at school, such strategies are essential for directing attention, for ensuring effective communication, and for establishing a foundation for learning about language and the world. They provide some of the essential building blocks for later, more complex learning and interaction.

SOCIAL INTERACTIONS: FOUNDATIONS FOR LEARNING

An important part of any child's development is the learning of the roles, rules, attitudes, and values of the community. This begins in the earliest parent–child interactions and provides a foundation for social interactions with others. The parent–child bond also gives the child a secure base for exploration, from which she can learn about the world on her own—eventually leading to self-esteem and self-confidence. Unfortunately, hearing mothers tend to be overprotective and controlling with their deaf children, constantly trying to help or direct their deaf child's play with toys and interactions with other children. They also tend to use more physical punishment with deaf than hearing children. Interestingly, the better the communication between mothers and their deaf children, the less physical punishment they use—likely because they need less.

Mothers' tendencies to control activities of their young deaf children have several sources. Most obviously, they simply may be trying to establish lines of communication. If they do not have an effective means of communicating with their deaf children, they might just be seeking to protect their children from harm or believe (sometimes accurately, sometimes not) that their children are unable to do

BOX 5.1
INTERACTING WITH YOUNG DEAF CHILDREN

To get and keep a young deaf child's attention:

- Use facial expressions and body language to appear "interesting"
- Use hand and body movements within their line of sight (to "break" their gaze)
- Touch the child gently to interrupt other activities
- Point to interesting things (and look at them yourself)

To facilitate communication and vocabulary learning:

- Point to things and *then* say what they are (and point again)
- Wait until the child is looking before communicating
- Slow down the rate of communication
- Don't make the child frequently shift attention away from something interesting
- Use short utterances
- Position yourself and objects within the child's visual field
- Ensure that hands (if signing) or face (if speaking) is in the child's visual field
- Begin *and* end utterances with important information (e.g., *The dog, he's brown isn't he, the dog?*)
- When referring to things, make signs or gestures on or near the objects
- Exaggerate, repeat, and prolong signs to make sure they are seen and recognized
- If child does not understand what is being said, don't just repeat it, restate it in a different way
- Allow more time for children to understand messages, especially in visually or acoustically noisy situations.

things for themselves. Alternatively they might be trying to compensate for feelings of inadequacy or powerlessness in dealing with their young deaf child, or they may just feel frustrated. In any case, such behaviors can result in a self-fulfilling prophecy. That is, children who do not have opportunities to explore and discover for themselves are likely to become more dependent on their parents and other adults. Alternatively, they might go about their exploration at inappropriate times or places and end up getting punished, injured, or lost. Most early intervention programs teach parents to avoid overcontrol and intrusiveness by "loosening up" and letting their child explore and experiment. But it is a hard habit to break.

EARLY INTERVENTION

We noted in Chapter 1 that *early intervention* is an important predictor of deaf children's successes in all areas of development, including education. That might make you think that early intervention is just for children. Actually, it is just as important for the parents of young deaf children, and many of those programs are now instead referred to as *parent–infant programs*. With recognition that having a deaf child changes the life of the entire family, there also has been a recent emphasis on *family-centered* programs. These programs are available in many communities through schools for the deaf, hospital outreach services, and local government agencies. Parents usually will learn about them at the time of newborn hearing screening.

The goal of early intervention programs is to start as early as possible to give deaf children the kinds of experiences they need with regard to language, parent–child interaction, social-emotional growth, and support for residual hearing. At the same time, interventionists provide parents with strategies for enhancing their child's development, building on their strengths, and adjusting to their needs. This kind of opportunity is especially important for deaf children with hearing parents (and for those parents), who are unlikely to have smooth and natural interactions, at least at the beginning. Language is not the only issue here, although it is perhaps the most important one. Regardless of whether they are oriented toward spoken language or sign language, intervention programs help to establish effective communication between parents and their deaf child in the context of day-to-day activities, thus fostering child learning and parent confidence. The result is greater parental involvement (but less intrusiveness) in their children's activities, a situation that supports social-emotional functioning, early language development, and later academic achievement.

Speaking of sign language and spoken language, ideally, early interventionists would not have preconceived ideas about whether any particular child should be raised with one or the other. Rather, children should be exposed to both, allowing them to grow with whatever mode or modes come most naturally and successfully. This may seem counterintuitive, but there is no evidence that being exposed to both causes any confusion or difficulty for either deaf or hearing children. Deaf children's early expressive (production) language skills, whether in sign or in speech, have been found to lead to better spoken language. Given that it is easier for younger children to acquire sign language than spoken language, there is no reason why they should not be exposed to both. Even children with cochlear implants appear to benefit from sign language in addition to speech, both in their language development and their later academic achievement. Early intervention

Box 5.2
WHAT TO LOOK FOR IN AN EARLY INTERVENTION PROGRAM

- No bias toward spoken language or sign language, but offering both
- Regular language reassessment
- Parent and family programs
- Educational programming, not just play
- An established curriculum
- Support for amplification and communication technologies
- Trained/certified staff

programs give deaf children the skills necessary to succeed when they enter formal schooling, either preschool or kindergarten (see Box 5.2). The long-term educational impact of various kinds of programs has not been fully investigated, but there is broad agreement about their social-emotional benefits, both at home and in school. Children enrolled in such programs show better self-control of their behavior, for example, something that influences their ability to pay attention in school as well as to begin and maintain friendships. These findings suggest that programs that provide a variety of language and nonlanguage opportunities for interpersonal interaction give children more diverse experiences and help them to deal with the necessities of growing up in a largely hearing world.

MOVING FROM HOME TO SCHOOL

Through their interactions with adults and peers, children come to learn who they are. Regardless of whether they are deaf or hearing, children seek the same kinds of emotional and practical support from others, learn the same kinds of behaviors, and are influenced by the same kinds of factors. Language, of course, plays a central role during this process (see later discussion). Explaining to deaf children why we (or others) behave the way we do allows them to acquire the rules of social interaction and better understand what is going on around them.

When deaf children enter school, they frequently move from a setting of considerable security and understanding, in both communication and interpersonal senses, to one that is relatively unknown and full of potential challenges. The rules of home and school often are different, and many deaf children do not have enough social experience or communication skills for the transition to be as smooth as it is for most hearing children. Preschool programs specifically designed to include deaf children are thus extremely useful in helping them to become ready for school, socially as well as academically.

Not surprisingly, the transition from home to school—and the social-emotional functioning that goes with it—is strongly affected by the quality of parent–child relationships. Controlling or overprotective behaviors on the part of hearing parents can lead their children to expect those kinds of behaviors from others. Parents and teachers who are constantly "rescuing" deaf children from awkward situations will prevent them from developing their own strategies for solving social problems. And, again, without a fully effective, shared communication system children may not give or receive the same social cues as hearing children. Research has shown that deaf children who are able to use both signed and spoken languages do better in the preschool classroom, because they are more likely to be understood by others. At the same time, more social "practice" with various children and adults offers young deaf children opportunities for learning at a variety of levels.

SOCIAL-EMOTIONAL GROWTH DURING THE SCHOOL YEARS

Deaf children from deaf families frequently are seen to have better social skills and greater self-esteem than deaf children coming from hearing families. In addition to having a wider range of social interactions and more effective communication skills, those children will have experienced greater understanding and acceptance from others (who are deaf) inside and outside the family. Deaf children of deaf parents also are more likely than those with hearing parents to have experienced consistent parenting behaviors from an early age, and interactions with (deaf) individuals outside of the immediate family are more likely to be similar to those within the family. Partly as a result, deaf children of deaf families tend to have a greater sense of being in control of their own lives. This *locus of control* is an important predictor of social as well as later academic and career success. Deaf children of hearing parents can be just as confident and secure as those of deaf parents, but it may require more conscious planning by their parents to ensure that they have sufficient personality-building experiences.

During the school years, deaf children encounter all of the same social problems and find the same social solutions as other children. Depending on their environments, they also might face additional challenges. In a public school setting, for example, being deaf makes them different; and parents who think being different in school does not matter are forgetting a lot about their own childhoods. The lack of acceptance that deaf students frequently find in mainstream programs may not affect their self-esteem, but it does affect their comfort and satisfaction with school. Deaf children in regular school classrooms often report feeling more isolated and lonely than students in schools or programs designed for deaf students, even if their parents think they are getting along just fine. In programs designed for deaf and hard-of-hearing children, they can find others who are like them, even if the hearing world is still all around them. Those programs therefore represent a fertile ground for social interactions with peers and deaf adults that go beyond what is available in most homes. They will offer deaf children more playmates and more communication during play than in public schools. They also are likely to be less overprotected and intruded upon by well-meaning adults.

Some of the benefits of the larger social circle gained in programs with other deaf students may seem trivial: things like going to the mall with a group of friends, telling jokes in the hallway, and flirting on the playground. But the importance of those behaviors for "normal" social and personality development during the school years cannot be ignored. If a deaf child is in a regular school, parents should consider seeking out other deaf and hard-of-hearing children for play dates, sports, or outings to interesting places.

Raising a child in a family that is not used to being visually oriented can be challenging for both parents and children. For example, regardless of whether parents decide to use a signed language or a spoken language, deaf children understand language better if they are looking at the person who is talking. This means both knowing who is talking and being able to see the person clearly. As any deaf or hard-of-hearing adult could explain, it is very difficult for a deaf child to follow group discussions in spoken language (with or without SimCom) because hearing people tend to "talk over each other," finishing each other's sentence and interrupting. Not only does this cause the deaf child to lose any thread of the conversation he might be hanging onto, but by the time he discovers that the speaker has changed (and who it is), he will have missed a lot of information.

Most deaf and hard-of-hearing adolescents and adults describe having experienced *dinner table syndrome*, where they had no idea what their family is talking about while all are laughing, connecting, and sharing history. Many deaf individuals come to dread holidays because of dinner table syndrome, and it is not unusual for children in residential schools for the deaf to ask whether they can stay there rather than going home for the holidays. Having attended holiday celebrations at schools and programs for deaf children and seeing the level of communication between some parents and children, we can understand why. Parents and siblings need to put forth all effort they can to make sure the communication environment is visually accessible, not only when addressing the deaf child. Seeing how adults talk to each other is one of the major ways that children learn how people communicate, negotiate, and share.

Even when families have a shared means of communication and thus can include their deaf and hard-of-hearing children in everyday activities, those children will still benefit from interacting with peers and role models who are like them. Peers and role models show children how to navigate the world as deaf or hard-of-hearing individuals. This is similar to how first-time mothers and immigrants often get together and share tips and their experiences. The sharing is reassuring and helpful. Parents should find local events for deaf and hard-of-hearing people in the community in order to expose their children to deaf role models. They also can look for summer camps (day or sleepover) for deaf and hard-of-hearing children. Participation in such events not only will be helpful for the child's self-esteem and social development, they will help parents better understand what it means to be deaf. Parents also will benefit from becoming involved in organizations for families of deaf children. These organizations host a variety of functions, provide parents and children with opportunities for interacting with similar families, and play an important advocacy role for deaf children and their families. For better or worse, some of these organizations have strong philosophical views about language and educational placement for deaf children. Others emphasize recognizing the individual differences among deaf and hard-of-hearing children and supporting them in whatever works best.

FINAL WORDS

Beyond similarities in their emotional reactions, parents vary considerably in their behaviors when they learn that they have a deaf child. Unless they are deaf themselves, understanding and accepting a child's hearing loss is never easy. Infants with hearing losses may respond differently to parents than children without hearing losses, and such differences in interactions often continue through adolescence at least. Parents and teachers may feel inadequate in dealing with a deaf child, and such feelings may lead them to inadvertently deny children valuable opportunities for exploration and experience.

There are two things hearing parents of deaf children should do as soon as possible: First, find an early intervention program where they can obtain information concerning hearing loss, assistive listening devices, communication, language development, and special education practices. Second, establish an effective means of communicating with your deaf child as soon as possible, keeping in mind that children benefit from different modes of communication and education. There is no single right answer for all deaf children.

The different experiences children have will affect how they view and interact with the world. In the case of deaf children of deaf parents, their fuller range of natural, everyday experiences often will lead to their passing through the various developmental stages at the same rate as hearing children. For deaf children of hearing parents, early experiences may not blend so readily into the background of family and community life. For both groups, the nature of their experiences may lead to differences in social, language, and perhaps academic functioning relative to hearing children.

Parents and teachers of deaf children often overlook the overwhelming amount of learning that takes place in informal interactions and activities both in and out of school. A large proportion of children's knowledge of the world, for example, comes from social studies, science, literature, and the like. To give these topics less attention than language-focused instruction assures that deaf children not only will have smaller vocabularies, but that the vocabularies they do develop will be relatively concrete and specific.

The intertwining of language, social, and cognitive development is fundamental to deaf children's construction of knowledge about the world and the way it works. Nurturing these developmental domains in home, school, and community activities must be one of our highest priorities. We also must make every effort to better understand how deaf children's development is influenced by different learning situations, rather than focusing on the traditional debates over the effects of hearing loss or the use of sign language on development and academic success. Most important, we cannot continue to assume that our deaf and hearing children will benefit in the same ways from similar interactions or instructional methods. As we describe in the next three chapters, the early experiences of deaf and hard-of-hearing children lead to some differences in how they learn and how they interact with the world. Only by recognizing and accommodating those differences can we offer them the best educational opportunities.

6

DEAF COGNITION

A PARENT OR teacher who has never encountered a deaf child before might ask, "How do deaf children learn if they can't hear?" This is essentially a question about deaf *cognition*, about whether deaf children think in words or signs (yes), whether they only remember things as pictures (no), and even whether brains work the same in deaf children and hearing children (yes and no). In studies of cognitive development, we also ask more specific questions about the effects of experience on various cognitive abilities, academic achievement, and a deaf child's *quality of life*. The answers to these questions provide insight into how to best raise and teach deaf children so as to take advantage of their strengths and compensate for any needs. In most cases, they tell us that deaf and hearing children are quite similar.

ARE DEAF CHILDREN AS SMART AS HEARING CHILDREN?

Discovering that their child is deaf is a traumatic experience for some parents, because many have never met a deaf adult, let alone a deaf doctor, lawyer, or college professor. When first learning about their child's hearing status, many believe that their child will always be isolated, will not be able to live independently, will never be smart. If you want to skip to the next section, the answer to this section's

title question is "yes." If you want to stay around, the rest of this section describes how we know that.

"Smartness" is a difficult thing to measure. Being smart involves both having acquired a lot of knowledge and having the ability to learn a lot more. When psychologists talk about *intelligence* (the technical term for "smartness"), they are referring to an individual's cognitive potential, including her ability to *learn* and *use* knowledge but not knowledge itself. The amount and quality of information that has been acquired is not a part of intelligence per se but reflects *achievement*. People with the same intellectual potential can have a wide range of knowledge or achievement depending on their environments and opportunities.

Actually, the question of whether deaf children are as intelligent as hearing children is not as simple as it might appear. Most tests developed to measure intelligence are intended for individuals who depend on hearing for most of their learning, and many intelligence tests and tests of specific cognitive abilities require hearing to complete the tasks. Such tests may be valid tests of intelligence for hearing children, but not for deaf children. For deaf children, those tests are measuring hearing first and cognition second. Other tests require spoken responses and a child who does not speak (or speak well) cannot be evaluated fairly.

When evaluated using intelligence tests that are fair for both hearing and speaking children, the two groups generally perform equally well. However, there may be different patterns of scores on parts of the test corresponding to cognitive abilities in which deaf or hearing individuals have an advantage (for example, mental imagery [deaf] or memory for sequences [hearing]). Recognizing that deaf and hearing children have equal intellectual potential even while differing on some dimensions relevant to learning is thus an essential aspect of raising and educating deaf children. Therefore, most of this chapter and the next two will consider this issue.

When we say that deaf and hearing learners are equally intelligent, we mean that how well children hear does not affect their ability to learn. As we saw in Chapter 3, the deaf population does have a larger proportion of individuals with learning challenges as a result of the etiologies (causes) of their deafness. Those children may require special education accommodations beyond those discussed here. Because their needs are so individual and vary so widely, there is little research that allows us to draw any general conclusions. This situation is regrettable, because children with multiple challenges usually are also in need of multiple educational accommodations (see Suggestions for Further Reading at the back of the book). In general, though, we do know quite a bit about deaf children's intellectual abilities, information that should help us to support their learning.

As we talk about these issues in the sections that follow, we often will distinguish between *intentional* and *incidental* learning. Intentional learning is what happens in situations in which a child either is given information by someone else or gets it for herself (for example, from a book, a game, or another person) with the goal of remembering or using the information later. Incidental learning, in contrast, refers to the "accidental" learning that goes on all the time simply by virtue of being awake and interacting with the world (for example, when reading a book for pleasure). All children learn incidentally about how the world works just by playing and observing things and people. Hearing children do a lot of incidental learning by overhearing what is going on around them, even if they are busy doing (and looking at) something else. Deaf children, in contrast, cannot overhear the conversations of others and have to shift their visual attention in order to "eavesdrop" using their eyes. Does that mean that hearing children learn more incidentally than deaf children? Maybe.

DO DEAF INDIVIDUALS SEE BETTER?

Many believe that blind people must hear better than sighted people and that deaf people must see better than hearing people. This notion of *sensory compensation* appears to be based on the assumption that we have a limited amount of perception capability, and that if it is not being used for one thing, it can be used for another. In fact, if one sense is partially or completely absent, there are three possibilities: (1) the remaining senses take over some of that capability and so they improve; (2) lacking input from one of the senses, the others do not develop or function as well as they could; or (3) it doesn't make any difference to the other senses.

Studies conducted since the 1980s suggest that perhaps all of these alternatives are true in some areas and to some extent. In the case of deaf individuals, this does not mean that they have Superman's super vision; people who are deaf actually are more likely to need glasses than people who are hearing. Nevertheless, deaf individuals—and sometimes even hearing individuals who use sign language—do show advantages over hearing individuals in several visual abilities. This is ultimately related to differences in the way that their brains work, but in terms of the behavior we see, it relates to differences in the way they use their visual attention. As we will describe later, changes in visual attention appear to be a natural adaptation to having to depend on vision rather than on vision and hearing together. They also are a natural part of deaf children becoming more visually oriented individuals. Because most deaf children are raised in hearing families, those visual skills usually have to be incidentally learned and may not develop fully. To reach their full visual potential, we often have to teach deaf children how to become visual learners.

Cognitive scientists and neuroscientists have conducted studies on visual processing in both animals and humans who were born deaf or became deaf. In human studies, deaf individuals who were born to deaf parents are the most interesting. As mentioned in Chapter 4, deaf children of deaf parents achieve the same early language development milestones as hearing children and because their hearing status usually is inherited, most do not have accompanying *neurological* (brain-related) problems or learning challenges. The study of these children therefore allows researchers to determine which cognitive differences are the result of not hearing (*auditory deprivation*), rather than language delays or other factors. Studies that also include native-signing hearing children of deaf parents provide information concerning the effects of sign language on cognitive development, separate from auditory deprivation.

Research involving these groups has shown that the visual abilities of deaf and hearing individuals are much the same. Both groups have similar abilities to notice differences between brighter and darker images and between different temporal (time) patterns in visually presented material, two common measures of basic visual processing. At higher levels of complexity, however, there are some real differences between deaf and hearing individuals. Consider, for example, paying attention to visual information presented to the *central visual field*—basically what you see right in front of you—compared to the *peripheral visual field*—what you see out of the "corner of your eye." Deaf individuals notice more quickly than hearing individuals when something appears in the peripheral visual field or if it moves.

They are also faster at shifting their visual attention to the periphery and then shifting it back. These abilities are the brain's way of adapting to being deaf, allowing deaf individuals a way of being alerted to danger and to others trying to communicate with them (visually). At the same time, however, they also carry the potential disadvantage of making deaf children more distractible in the classroom, where multiple (visual) things can be happening at the same time. This might explain results of a study involving deaf high school students that found that the students visually attended to the signing of the teacher and their classmates less than 50% of the time. Whether the students were prone to distraction or had not yet mastered the attentional skills involved in being visual learners, those results provide one reason why deaf students often lag behind hearing students in the classroom. At a practical level, the results suggest that educational settings including deaf children should avoid open-landscaping classrooms and organize desks and chairs so that they are all facing toward the teacher.

The increased sensitivity of peripheral vision among deaf children with signing deaf parents is not affected or caused by their use of sign language. We know that because deaf individuals who use spoken language rather than sign language can acquire the same abilities as those raised with sign language. One recent study observed deaf teachers trying to help deaf preschool children to acquire visual attention skills. Although their study did not include hearing teachers, the deaf teachers were found to pay special attention to encouraging such skills in deaf children of hearing parents, apparently assuming that deaf children of deaf parents acquire them incidentally at home.

Eventually, deaf children learn when they can look away from a signer—perhaps after seeing enough of a sign to know what it will be—without missing what is being said. Early on, this behavior appears to be less frequent in deaf children of hearing parents than in deaf children of deaf parents, but our own research has shown that even deaf children with hearing parents have that ability by the time they get to college. Furthermore, the advantage in peripheral vision seen in deaf college students is also found in hearing college students who play a lot of video games. So it's not really a "deaf effect" so much as learning to use peripheral vision.

In summary, deaf individuals do not really "see" better than hearing individuals, but they can better attend to what occurs visually around them. If they are not taught how to use their visual attention effectively by parents and teachers, this cognitive difference might lead only to greater distractibility and not be utilized for learning. It is essential that deaf and hard-of-hearing children gain visual learning skills, regardless of how much their hearing benefits from cochlear implants or hearing aids.

DOES SIGN LANGUAGE HAVE AN EFFECT ON COGNITION?

Around the world each year there are increasing numbers of children and adults learning sign language. Parents of hearing children are now purchasing sign language books and DVDs to teach their infants how to sign.[1] Some countries do not have instructional materials in their native sign language, so parents in those countries purchase materials in American Sign Language (ASL) or the sign language of a neighboring country, even though deaf individuals in their country do not use that language. The reason parents are teaching their hearing infants and toddlers to sign is that they believe it will enhance their child's cognitive abilities—and it does, at least to some extent.

Learning how to sign does not increase a child's intelligence. Intelligence is composed of many different cognitive functions and represents the individual's overall capacity to learn. But some of those functions do improve with sign language practice. These include memory for visual-spatial information and locations in space as well as the mental generation and manipulation of mental images. For example, imagine a capital letter "Z" and turn it onto its right side. What do you "see"? Deaf people generally can do that faster than hearing people can.

Signers also pay more attention to facial expressions and are better able to recognize familiar faces compared to nonsigners (remember from Chapter 4 that sign language is not all on the hands). In addition, signers show some improvement in visual-motor coordination and speed, for example, in assembling blocks to create a particular visual pattern. (It would be interesting to see whether they are also faster in completing jigsaw puzzles.) So not only does sign language help deaf children to communicate with others and learn about the world, it has more subtle benefits as well.

COGNITIVE DEVELOPMENT AND LANGUAGE

Research studies involving deaf children that give the clearest results usually examine very specific cognitive abilities, and therefore they are often uninteresting to people other than the researchers themselves. Even if it seems boring, this level of analysis is important because of the complex relationship between language and cognitive development for both deaf and hearing children. We will only scratch the surface of this issue here, dividing our discussion into three parts. The first section considers the impact of language development on the development of the *executive functions*—the most advanced and complicated aspect of cognitive

functioning. The next section looks at language in the social parts of cognitive development, or *social cognition*. The third section then considers the potential impact on cognitive development of learning two languages and learning through two languages—*bilingualism* and *bilingual education*.

Higher Level Cognitive Functions

The highest level of cognitive activity is called *executive functioning*. The executive functions control lower level cognitive activities such as attention, learning, and memory. They include *metacognition* (thinking about thinking or cognition about cognition) and *behavioral regulation* such as the control of emotions, thoughts, and behaviors. Language acts like an orchestra conductor for the executive functions, making it possible for the brain to have control over its instruments. Current research suggests that language fluency is necessary for optimal executive function development, and children with poor language skills will be limited in several cognitive domains as a result.

Among both deaf and hearing children, language delays can cause distractibility, *impulsivity* (acting without thinking), difficulty with emotional control and organization, and behavioral problems. Many of these difficulties are also found in children with attention-deficit/hyperactivity disorder (ADHD). ADHD can be caused by the same things that cause hearing loss, and deaf children are somewhat more likely to have ADHD than hearing children. Often, however, deaf children are misdiagnosed as having ADHD when they show ADHD-like behaviors due to their lack of language ability and executive functioning. Imagine being a child with limited language skills sitting in a classroom where everyone is talking (in either sign or speech). It would be hard to sit still and conform to the classroom behaviors if you do not know what is going on or what people are saying.

The executive functions take longer to develop than other cognitive abilities. Most of the development occurs during the first 13 years of life, but it continues at least until early adulthood. The fact that many deaf children show increasing delays in age-appropriate language as they get older means that there also may be increasing delays in executive functioning. Children need to be in rich language environments for the executive functions to develop naturally and for them to gain age-appropriate abilities and behaviors. Yet many deaf children are raised in language environments that are not fully accessible. The resulting variability in deaf children's language abilities requires considerable variety in language programming. Both the cost to schools of offering several different language alternatives and the understandable preference of most parents to have their children share their own (spoken) language can result in missed opportunities for language and cognitive growth, and for executive functioning in particular.

The need for efficient executive functioning increases as children get older and the classroom becomes less structured, thus requiring more internal resources, control, and organization. The executive functions are perhaps most obviously needed when a child approaches a novel task with minimal support from other people, a situation in which both intelligence and prior knowledge are important. The brain has to figure out what to do. Over time, the more frequently children are faced with novel tasks, the better they get at problem solving. In fact, *intelligence* is sometimes defined as being able to apply prior knowledge to novel situations (see Chapter 8). As we have seen, however, deaf children often find themselves raised in overly structured environments at home and at school, frequently receiving more assistance in problem solving than their same-aged peers, regardless of whether they need it. The more structure provided by parents and teachers, the less deaf children will have to figure things out for themselves. Environments that are too structured therefore do not encourage executive function development or, for that matter, a child's self-confidence and self-esteem. If we want deaf children to develop cognitive flexibility and become independent learners, we need to let them tackle (appropriate) challenges themselves. This is not only true in the classroom, it also applies to other learning contexts and to social interactions.

Theory of Mind and Social Interaction

A child's understanding of the social world tells us a lot about the relationship between language development and executive functioning. One area of study involving language, executive functioning, and social cognition is *theory of mind*, that is, knowing that other people have thoughts, emotions, beliefs, and so on. Theory of mind usually is illustrated using the *false-belief task*. Imagine a researcher sitting in front of two 8-year-olds. With them watching, the experimenter places a piece of candy under a box on the table. Then, the experimenter asks one of the children to leave the room. After the child leaves, the experimenter moves the candy from under the box and into a basket. The experimenter then asks the child remaining in the room, "Where does he (pointing to the child out of the room) *think* the candy is?" or "Where will he look for the candy?" The correct answer, of course, is "in the box," even though the candy is now in the basket. Theory of mind thus includes one's ability to ignore appearances and think about what someone else might be thinking.

Theory of mind development is necessary for age-appropriate communication, learning, and social interaction. Deaf children, however, often lag behind hearing peers in theory of mind, at least as indicated by the false-belief task. Recent research has clarified those findings, showing that deaf children of deaf parents develop theory of mind just like hearing children of hearing parents, and that deaf children whose hearing parents sign to them show better theory of mind abilities than those who depend on spoken language. Normal theory of mind development therefore appears to depend on effective parent–child communication and parents' ability to explain emotional and other cognitive states in the context of their causes and outcomes. That's how children "learn" what is going on in other people's minds. It is also how they come to figure out what people mean when they say things indirectly, such as "It's cold in here" when they actually mean "Close the door." Once again, we see the importance of full, early access to language for deaf as well as hearing children.

Bilingualism and Cognitive Functioning

Bilingual programming in deaf education—being taught both the sign language of the Deaf community and the written language of the hearing community as equal partners—is relatively new, and like many other practices in deaf education the evidence is not yet in concerning its impact on cognitive functioning and academic outcomes. There is a wealth of evidence, however, indicating that bilingualism can have a positive impact on cognitive functioning in hearing children (as early as 7 months of age), and many people assume that the same will be true with deaf children.

We noted earlier that the executive functions, like other cognitive abilities, adjust to the demands of the environment. Because bilinguals have to focus on one language and block the other language in order to deal with everyday activities, this part of their executive functioning is better than what we see in people with only one language. Similar results are obtained in nonverbal tasks, indicating that bilingualism offers general cognitive advantages beyond language itself. Focusing and blocking skills, in particular, would be extremely useful for deaf children, helping them to avoid visual and other distractions. Rather than viewing bilingual education as a last resort, we need to recognize the possibility that two languages for deaf children might be better than one, just as they are for hearing children.

FINAL WORDS

The primary take-home message of this chapter is that being deaf or hard of hearing need not negatively affect cognitive development. Delayed access to language can have far-reaching consequences, however, and most deaf children are raised and taught in environments where they have limited access to language. Deaf children need to be immersed in language as early as possible and throughout childhood for cognitive development to proceed naturally and normally.

A second message to be taken away from this chapter is that it is important to help deaf children become visually oriented learners; they cannot necessarily do it by themselves. Deaf children focus visually on a wider scan of the environment than hearing children, carrying potential advantages and disadvantages. Only by recognizing that they are different in this way can we teach deaf children to take advantage of their visual skills (even when listening to spoken language).

Sign language does not interfere with the development of spoken language or any other aspect of development. The benefits of knowing two languages over only one have been well documented among individuals with two spoken languages and for hearing children acquiring sign language in addition to spoken language. Such findings will say to some that "sign language is the way to go." The truth is that any way one can maximize a deaf child's access to fluent language is the way to go. Just because parents are speaking does not mean their child will understand their speech. And if parents' signing is inconsistent, their child won't understand that either. Comprehensive assessment and regular monitoring of deaf children's communication skills and language development are essential, as is a willingness to provide "whatever works."

Deaf children who have full access to language throughout development will be those with the most flexible cognitive skills and the greatest potential for learning. They will be able to think hypothetically, considering their actions and potential consequences before they act. Therefore, they will also be better able to understand others and different points of view. They will be able to solve complex problems in their heads and have a good idea of how to approach new problems that might be beyond their experience. They will be better students and ultimately become independent learners, able to lead more productive lives and have a better quality of life. They will also be smarter.

7

LEARNING AND MEMORY

CHAPTER 6 INTRODUCED the cognitive development of deaf children and ways in which it is affected by the environments in which they grow up. As we saw, because of their primary reliance on visual rather than auditory experience in language and in other interactions with people, the cognitive foundations of learning among deaf children are somewhat different than those of hearing children. Our understanding of the way that deaf children interact with the world—essentially our view of their cognitive functioning —has always influenced the way that people think they should be educated, regardless of whether that understanding was accurate.

The aforementioned situation has had a great influence on deaf learners for centuries, but there are two issues of particular relevance to parents and teachers today. One is that there are some Deaf adults who view their educational histories, including their parents' and teachers' obsessions with spoken language, as a form of oppression, if not abuse. As often as not, however, the people who voice such views are hearing people rather than deaf people, or deaf people talking about the lives of others rather than their own. It is difficult to convince such individuals that most parents and teachers have always done their best to educate deaf children, but that society has long been ignorant about the potential of children with any disability—not just those who are deaf. The second consequence of the cognition-education linkage is that as our understanding of cognitive psychology and cognitive development has grown, the education of deaf children has become more *evidence based* (shown by research to be effective) and tailored to their strengths and needs.

Within the field of psychology, the shift away from viewing children's learning as essentially the same as that of pigeons and rats did not occur until the late 1960s. That change from an emphasis on external behavior (referred to as *behaviorism*) to an emphasis on what goes on in the mind (*cognitive psychology*) was occurring at the same time that we were learning that the gestural systems used by deaf individuals in the United States and elsewhere were really *language*. Both shifts reflected changes in society and science consistent with the times, and it will be worth briefly considering the intertwining of psychology and deaf education that brought us to where we are today—and led to this book.

COGNITION AND LEARNING: FROM DARKNESS TO ENLIGHTENMENT

The historical connection between views of deaf children's cognitive abilities and their learning can be seen as involving three or four historical stages. The first stage, which has been referred to as *the deaf as inferior*, resulted from work in the early 1900s that seemed to show that deaf children were not as intelligent as their hearing peers. It was during this time that psychologists studying intelligence first developed *nonverbal intelligence tests* precisely so that they could measure the intelligence of deaf children. We understand today that much of that research was influenced by the researchers' (and society's) belief that spoken language was an essential component of human intelligence. Nevertheless, some of their findings, like deaf children's difficulty in remembering sequences of items that are not meaningfully connected, are still obtained and will be discussed later in this chapter and the next. Today, however, we have a much better understanding of what those results really mean.

The second stage in thinking about cognition and learning among deaf children has been labeled *the deaf as concrete*. From the 1940s to the early 1960s, research on deaf children's problem-solving and literacy skills was interpreted to indicate that they were doomed to be concrete and literal, living in the here and now, with little ability for abstract thinking. At the time, most psychologists believed that deaf people who did not speak did not have any language, and they failed to recognize that it was the way that we were teaching deaf children and limiting their early experience—and not their hearing loss—that was responsible for many of the research findings and observed academic limitations. While deaf children are no longer seen as being less capable of abstract thought than hearing children, teachers continue to struggle with deaf children's tendencies to behave in apparently concrete ways in academic and social situations. We will consider the reasons for that kind of behavior in this chapter and in Chapter 8.

It was not until the 1970s that psychologists and educators arrived at the point that is referred to as *the deaf as intellectually normal*. Armed with the new cognitive psychology and a refined understanding of intelligence, researchers began to examine relations among cognition, language, and learning in deaf and hearing children. Rather than seeing deaf children as lacking something, they finally recognized the influence of deaf children's early language and social experiences on their development and showed that, in terms of intelligence, they were quite normal.

We now know that deaf children are just as capable of learning as are their hearing peers, and that being deaf does not result in any insurmountable educational barriers. In essence, people have come to accept that *difference does not mean deficiency*—the newest stage in our understanding of the cognition-learning linkage in deaf children. In this view, the one that we have emphasized throughout this book, deaf and hearing learners may vary in their approaches to various tasks, differ in their means of communication, and have different knowledge organized in different ways without such differences being either good or bad. This perspective has led us to examine differences between deaf and hearing students as a way to better understand the intellectual development of deaf children and optimize their experiences

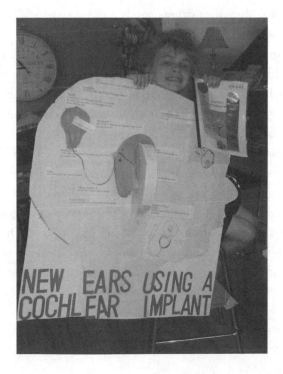

in educational settings. It is with that perspective that we now examine learning and memory in deaf children.

Before we get started, we should point out that learning is different from memory, although both are a part of the same whole. *Learning* is the acquisition of new knowledge, whereas *memory* refers to the storage and retrieval of knowledge. *Knowledge* is used broadly here to mean information not only about things and ideas but also skills, such as how to type or ride a bicycle, and extremely complex skills like reading. The rest of this chapter will examine some of what we know, think we know, and do not know about how deaf students learn, store, and retrieve information and skills. In Chapter 8, we will look at the organization of that information in the mind/brain and how it is used in problem solving. Meanwhile, we will focus on the processes by which information gets into memory, that is, *learning*. Then we will be in a position to consider how information in memory—what has been learned—is used.

LEARNING

One would expect that a chapter about deaf children's learning would explain how deaf children learn. Readers who have read the previous chapters, however, will recognize that we already have discussed learning in a variety of settings, beginning essentially at birth. They also will realize that questions like "How will deafness affect my child's ability to learn?" are far more complex than they might seem. The key here will be understanding the foundations of learning in terms of the knowledge and skills that deaf children bring to the learning context and how parents and teachers teach children to utilize them. That is, what do deaf children need to have in order to take advantage of educational opportunities and interventions, and how can we tailor our instructional methods and materials to support them?

In seeking answers to these questions, parents and teachers often ask how deaf learners compare to hearing learners. Some people in our field believe that this is an inappropriate question and we should instead focus on deaf children's strengths and perhaps differences among deaf children as a function of language skills, school placement, parental hearing status, and so on. Such an approach might make sense if we were dealing with deaf children alone, but in a world where most deaf children have to compete in mainstream classrooms, it is essential that we understand ways in which their learning, knowledge, and educationally relevant skills differ from the hearing children who will sit beside them.

One thing we cannot deny is that deaf children rely more on vision for learning than do hearing children. We described in Chapter 6 how deaf and hearing individuals

BOX 7.1
VISION HELPS HEARING PEOPLE TO UNDERSTAND SPEECH

Hearing individuals rely more on vision than they realize, and they even use it in comprehending spoken language. The British psychologist Harry McGurk demonstrated this phenomenon in a now classic experiment. To understand the *McGurk effect*, first say the words "bet," "debt," and "get" to yourself several times. The only difference in the way the three words are spoken is where they begin in the mouth: the front, the middle, and the back. McGurk presented individuals with a video of a face saying the letter /b/ while the soundtrack produced a /g/ sound. The result was that hearing subjects heard the middle sound /d/. That is, the combination of "seeing" one sound and hearing another averaged out to hearing the one in the middle! In essence, this showed that hearing people rely on visual processing of lip movements even while they *listen* to what individuals say. Hearing individuals also use visual processing of facial expressions and the gestures people make when they talk, although they may not be as aware of it as deaf individuals.

differ in aspects of visual attention. Sometimes while driving, hearing people will turn down their car stereos to be able to see street signs better, and some say they can hear better with their glasses on. Apparently, hearing can interfere with or help with visual processing (see Box 7.1).

Deaf individuals generally are more sensitive to visual information than are hearing individuals and have some related advantages. Not only is it unnecessary for them to turn down the music when they need to pay careful (visual) attention, but they notice visual information in the environment that hearing individuals do not. Visual information in a learning environment also may be important for deaf students even when it is not for hearing students. In interpersonal interactions, such information might include things like gestures and facial expressions, and eye, mouth, and body movements. Pictures accompanying text, the spatial layout of objects, and visual characteristics of people (like emotions) and things (like colors) also are likely to be more readily noticed by and more important to deaf students than hearing students, supporting their learning where hearing students depend on hearing. Some of those features will be irrelevant, however, so deaf children have to learn what kinds of visual information they should attend to in different situations.

Gesture, for example, is an innate aspect of communication, and even individuals who are born totally blind gesture when they speak (not to mention hearing people using cell phones, where the person they are talking to can't see them). How often hearing children gesture when they are between 1 and 4 years old is a predictor of the size of their vocabularies later, and gestures are assumed to be an important building block of language for both hearing and deaf toddlers. Studies of the gestures used by deaf and hearing children have found them to use similar gestures in similar contexts, although deaf children tend to use gesture more often and more creatively. Learning to recognize the importance of such visual signals therefore is especially important and relevant to deaf learners—one more way in which they are visual learners.

Visual Learning

Babies born with less than normal hearing quickly learn to pay attention to the visual world: looking at facial movements of their caregivers, their gestures, and where they are looking—perhaps even before their caregivers realize the baby is deaf. Although it is unclear exactly how that visual learning proceeds, their visual processing skills (and the parts of their brains that deal with vision) consequently will develop somewhat differently than hearing babies for whom sights and sounds are usually connected.

Some scientists and practitioners claim that an emphasis on visual learning for babies with reduced hearing sensitivity might hinder their auditory learning. Consistent with this view, auditory-verbal approaches to speech therapy (see Chapter 4) often include covering the speaker's mouth so deaf and hard-of-hearing children have to learn to rely entirely on whatever hearing they have. Alternatively, it might turn out to be useful to turn off children's hearing aids and cochlear implants so they can practice their visual learning skills. Yet, because of the strong emphasis on auditory learning rather than visual learning among parents and speech-language professionals, we actually know less about visual learning among deaf babies and young children than we do for hearing children.

Deaf parents, of course, raise their deaf children to be visual learners. They do so without thinking about it through their natural, everyday interactions. Hearing parents, in contrast, do not know what it is like to be raised as a visual learner, and it is not surprising that they are often relatively unskilled in creating an information-rich environment for their young deaf children based on vision. This is one thing that parents learn in parent-infant early intervention programs, and we have seen some teachers of the deaf "teaching" deaf children how to direct their own visual attention and gain the attention of others.

As discussed in Chapter 6, being deaf leads to children attending more to the visual periphery, therefore widening their *learning visual field*. This adaptation is important because it makes them more visually aware of what is happening around them. Their greater sensitivity to movement in the periphery offers opportunities for incidental learning, just as the attention of hearing children is attracted by what they hear going on around them. Over time, the greater distractibility of young deaf children created by that sensitivity will be offset by their ability to rapidly shift visual attention away from and back to the person or thing of central interest. Exactly how this happens has not been documented, but there are clearly big individual differences in when and how well different children come to achieve that balance.

Auditory Learning

Most of the research involving auditory learning among deaf children is relatively recent, focusing on those with cochlear implants. While hearing aids and implants can help children hear better, children who use them still have to rely more on vision than do their hearing peers. For them, visual and auditory learning can work together, providing mutually supporting or redundant sources of information. Auditory information can help them speechread, draw their attention to visual information in the environment, and provide additional information about people and things. As we suggested earlier, this could mean that *simultaneous communication* (see Chapter 3) would be beneficial for children with cochlear implants, but the issue has not yet been explored in any depth.

A variety of studies on auditory learning and memory among children with cochlear implants has been conducted, comparing them to hearing children. That research has not included deaf children who do not utilize implants, so it is difficult to draw any conclusions about deaf children in general. Nevertheless, children with cochlear implants typically show shorter memory spans for auditory information because the speed of their internal speech (involved in memory *rehearsal*), like their external speech, is slower than that of hearing children. That finding also is obtained when colored lights or pictures are used instead of words, indicating that children with implants tend to label nonverbal material during learning and memory tasks, just like hearing children.

Taken together, such studies indicate that early hearing supports children's learning how to combine information into larger units. This ability is important, but it also is relatively fragile and easily disrupted. This might explain why even minimal hearing losses can affect children's reading, a skill that is heavily dependent on combining letter/sound and meaning units into words and phrases. Without a comparison to deaf children who do not use implants, it is unclear exactly how much cochlear implants affect this kind of information processing in deaf children. Still, just as earlier implantation generally leads to better hearing, language, and speech than later implantation, it apparently also leads to better learning and memory for both auditory and visual sequential information (see Box 7.2).

BOX 7.2
LANGUAGE AND MEMORY: ESSENTIAL OR ACCIDENTAL?

Language, thinking, and memory often seem to be closely linked, but it is not always clear whether that connection is necessary. For example, try counting silently to yourself, backwards, from 97, by threes (97, 94, 91...). Most people (including many deaf people) have the sensation of moving their vocal apparatus (tongues and mouths), even if their mouths are closed. But is that just a habit? What about the drunkard who is overheard saying, "Now just put the key right there into that little hole in the doorknob..."? Is his language guiding his action, or is it just because he is drunk? When it comes to memory, *rehearsal*—saying something over and over again to yourself—is one of the most effective tools for retaining short lists (telephone numbers, shopping lists, and so on). Rehearsal is also one of the first memory strategies acquired by young children. On average, it first appears in deaf and hard-of-hearing children later than it does in hearing children, if you consider chronological age. Alternatively, if you consider the number of years that a child has had full, effective access to language (for example, through sign language or a cochlear implant), rehearsal emerges after the same number of "language years" in deaf and hard-of-hearing and hearing children.

Measuring (School) Learning

In school, deaf children's learning, like hearing children's learning, is usually evaluated in terms of the grades they receive on tests, classroom work, and projects, as well as in overall yearly grades. Assessment of children's *achievement*, in contrast, typically relies on standardized tests. A variety of studies during the 1970s reported that deaf children with deaf parents scored higher on achievement tests than did deaf children with hearing parents (even if they still lag behind hearing children). Many people have concluded that such advantages were the result of early access to sign language, but that now appears not to be the case. As we will see in Chapter 9 with regard to reading, parents who are able to provide their deaf children with effective access to through-the-air communication—signed or spoken—and to written language have children who are the best readers. It doesn't matter if those parents are deaf or hearing. In addition, two of the best predictors of deaf students' academic achievement are parents' acceptance of their child's hearing loss and their having high expectations for their children. These two attitudes may be more frequent in deaf parents than hearing parents, but they need not be. Involvement in their children's learning and effective parent–child communication are what is important. Those we can change; parental hearing status we cannot.

Whatever else might be involved in achievement testing, we should point out that deaf children from immigrant families have an added difficulty. In the United States and Canada, for example, such children frequently have to learn both English and American Sign Language at the same time, while using another language (or two) at home. This is a particular challenge for teachers and schools in larger cities, where a single classroom might have deaf students with almost as many different home languages as there are students. For the child, parents may be less able to help with homework, and opportunities for exposure to the language of instruction may be more limited. Although there do not appear to be any specific studies on the topic, colleagues of ours who teach deaf children in Toronto and New York have told us that their immigrant students have greater difficulties in gaining English literacy skills than do other deaf children. In our own work at the college level, we have found that international deaf students lag behind both American deaf students and international hearing students in their classroom learning, even though they have acquired ASL and have sufficient English skills to score well on college entrance examinations. Perhaps these results are not surprising, but they point to the need for greater resources—and greater resourcefulness—in classrooms with deaf students who have different home languages.

If you were to look at published statistics, you would find that deaf children in mainstream settings typically obtain higher scores on achievement tests than do children in special schools. Those reports, however, do not take into account the fact that children who are enrolled in one kind of school setting or another are different to begin with, and that not all schools are equipped to handle deaf students—let alone those with disabilities. When such factors are taken into account, it turns out that what kind of school program deaf children attend explains less than 5% of variation in their academic achievement! Some of our own research, meanwhile, has shown that when deaf students are taught by experienced teachers of the deaf, they learn just as much as their hearing classmates, even if they come into the classroom with less knowledge of the topic that is being taught (see Chapter 11). From their own experience, those teachers have learned how deaf children think, what they know, and how best to support their learning. A large part of that involves students remembering what they have been taught and being able to retrieve it when necessary. So let us take a look at memory.

MEMORY

Deaf and hearing children can often remember things equally well, even though they differ in how they process new knowledge, store it, and find it again. In other cases, deaf and hearing children may remember the same *amount* of information but differ in *which* information they remember from something they have seen. We thus see again that the ways in which deaf children learn may not be the same as the ways hearing children learn.

Memory typically is described in terms of two components, *short-term memory* and *long-term memory*. If you stop and think about one of your elementary school teachers, you will be retrieving that information from your long-term memory and putting it into your short-term or *working memory*, the "workspace" where thinking goes on. Long-term memory, then, is where you keep all of your memories, knowledge, and skills. Short-term memory is where you have information that you are paying attention to right now. New information has to go through short-term memory to get into long-term memory. Sometimes it gets there, and sometimes it doesn't.

Generally speaking, deaf and hearing individuals are similar in how much information they recall in long-term memory tasks, but Chapter 8 will discuss differences in their memory performance as a result of the way they organize and use that information. Most memory research involving deaf adults and children, however, has focused on short-term memory, revealing several differences between deaf and hearing learners. Researchers are trying to figure out why there are those differences, but for the most part they do not seem to be the result of how much hearing one has. We have already seen that deaf learners vary greatly in their language experiences, language delays, and their reliance on sign language versus spoken language. All of those can have an impact on memory. Children and adults who are fluent in a signed language, for example, have been shown to have better visual-spatial memory, regardless of whether they are deaf or hearing.

Think about the card game Concentration, where cards are spread out and the task is to match up pairs, taking turns turning over only two cards at a time. Deaf signers have been found to be better than nonsigners in Concentration because of their better visual-spatial memory. We know that this must be the result of their use of a sign language rather than being deaf, because skilled hearing signers show the same advantage. Contrast this with the finding that both hearing individuals and "oral" deaf individuals have better memory than deaf signers for sequential memory tasks, like the *digit span* task in which a sequence of numbers has to be remembered both forward and backward. How much spoken language a deaf person has is related to her memory span in the same way that sign language skill affects visual-spatial memory.

Our description of the relative strengths of deaf and hearing children in visual-spatial and sequential memory should not be taken to indicate that either group is inept in "the opposite" kind of memory, or that either kind of memory is not important. Everyone has both visual-spatial memories (in the form of visual images) and verbal memories (in the form of language). Information that is remembered using two kinds of memory rather than one is typically remembered better. In educating deaf children, therefore, explaining pictures or diagrams with language will lead to better learning and memory than either one alone, just as it will with hearing children. For this reason, we continue to emphasize both the importance of language and the importance of deaf children becoming visual learners. Neither one is sufficient for optimal learning and academic achievement.

Findings like these remind us that the experiences that deaf children (and we) have growing up shape our memories and other cognitive processes at the same time that they are shaping our brains. While research has been very informative in describing such processes, it has not been very helpful in guiding teachers on how to make use of that information in the classroom. Importantly, differences between deaf and hearing learners in their memory spans and visual-spatial memory abilities do not mean that they differ in their memory *capacities* (how much information they can retain) or that we should not expect deaf children to memorize material in school. One of our early studies showed that deaf and hearing students have equal memory capacities, even if the two groups pay attention to or use different aspects of to-be-remembered information.

Presumably, we could increase deaf students' memory spans and hearing students' visual-spatial memories through explicit training. As far as we know, research has not yet explored how much or what kind of instruction would be required in the case of deaf children, but there have been numerous studies showing that it is possible to increase memory span and visual-spatial memory in hearing college students. More to the point, it is unclear whether such training for deaf children is necessary or whether the natural balance they develop in their cognitive skills is all they need to fully benefit from classroom instruction. If we were to spend a lot of classroom time retraining memory, the time available to other things would be reduced. It thus seems more helpful to educate teachers about how memory works in deaf and hearing children so that they can be sensitive to the strengths and weaknesses of each group. Of course, hearing teachers are generally aware of how memory works for hearing children, based on their own experience. The need for them to recognize and accommodate such cognitive differences among deaf children is one reason why we wrote this book.

FINAL WORDS

Over the last three chapters, we have seen that the early experiences of deaf and hearing children shape many of the "lower level" processes involved in development,

Question: I work as a sign language researcher in Iceland. I face the following problem: deaf immigrants who only know their sign language. They ask us which language to speak at home to their children, both deaf and hearing—our mother sign language, Icelandic sign language (in cases of deaf children of deaf immigrants), or Icelandic. For me the answer is: their mother sign language, and let the children do extra classes in Icelandic/Icelandic Sign Language. I understand also why they would like to use Icelandic Sign Language and even Icelandic, but I still am of the opinion that they should use their mother tongue at home. Are you familiar with literature on this particular issue?

Answer: This is a simple question with an answer that is really far too complex to do it justice on this forum. I will attempt the beginning of an answer. I am not actually aware of any literature that directly addresses this question, but it's one we deal with all the time (immigrants of all kinds, including signing deaf immigrants).

The literature on home vs. school language in *hearing* immigrants says that maintaining the home language is important for several reasons. First, maintaining a high level of competence in the mother tongue helps support the cognitive-linguistic development of the children in both the mother tongue and the new language. Relatedly, the way for the children to maintain a high level of competence in the mother tongue is for the parents (i.e., adult language users of that language) to continue to speak it, rather than a broken form of the new language, or if not broken, then not as competent a form of the new language. Secondly, the children are forced to live in the second language daily anyway, and they will learn it well, particularly if they are interacting in the spoken and written forms of that language. It may take a few years, but it will happen, barring a fundamental language learning disorder. That said, older children and teens will probably have more difficulty learning the second language, especially if they are not literate in their first language. However, children and teens who are literate in their mother tongue can use, to the extent that there are similarities between the written forms of the languages, their literacy knowledge to help them learn the second language. The whole issue is far more complex than "the younger the better" because very young children are typically not literate in their first language. However, very young children often learn their second language without an accent, and in the absence of (especially literate) support in their mother tongue, may even lose their first language.

In short, competent users of any language should maintain that language in the home. All the better if these competent users also know/learn the new language, because at some point, the kids' competence in the new language will overtake the mother tongue because they are being educated in the new language. The worst-case scenario is for the parents to stop speaking their own language and try to communicate in the new language; then their kids likely will end up with second-language competence in both languages—that is, no real native language.

building up more complex processes, from turn-taking to social interaction and from directing attention to remembering a teacher's instructions. Without providing details of how these processes work (an introductory psychology textbook will be useful for that purpose), we explained that learning how to interact with others, to understand what they want, and to control their own behavior naturally develops in deaf children just as it does in hearing children. Deaf children rely more on vision, and as they become visual learners, they will be better able to make effective use of visual processing across a variety of academic and interpersonal situations.

Although deaf children naturally have a greater reliance on vision, that does not mean they will become skilled visual learners naturally, without assistance from others. Learning to look in the direction that another person is looking in order to better understand what the person is talking about, recognizing the importance of facial and body movements to language comprehension, knowing where to look when, and balancing a greater sensitivity in peripheral vision with the ability to ignore distraction are all skills that are acquired over time. Deaf children may learn to do so incidentally, but explicit instruction or guidance will help make acquisition more rapid and more efficient.

Part of becoming a visual learner is learning to use vision to understand events and relations in the environment and to support memory. Information that is learned through language, either spoken language or sign language, will be remembered in the form of language to the same extent that it is among hearing children, at least in short-term or working memory. Long-term memory, in contrast, usually retains meaning rather than the precise form of the input, and whether something is learned through sign language, spoken language, print, or diagrams becomes less important. Learning is best, however, when it involves both verbal (but not necessarily vocal) and nonverbal information. It is therefore essential that deaf children acquire both language fluency and skill in visual learning strategies. Armed with those learning tools and the knowledge acquired through them, they can approach problem solving both in everyday situations and in the classroom.

8

PROBLEM SOLVING AND KNOWLEDGE

THIS CHAPTER LIES at the intersection of issues discussed in the previous five chapters, from the information that deaf children take from their various senses through their learning styles and their memory processes. In many ways, *learning* is always a problem-solving task regardless of whether it is from a book (reading), from a teacher's classroom presentation, or from watching how a neighbor plants a garden. That is, problem solving involves using existing knowledge and applying it to new situations to achieve some goal. So rereading a book like *The Cat in the Hat*, which a child might already have memorized, is not going to involve much problem solving, but reading a new book will, because some of the words are new and the content is new.

Playing a familiar board game like *Candyland* also will not involve problem solving unless new issues of following the rules or dealing with an unruly competitor crop up. But playing with the new kid who just moved in next door kid certainly will, and the problem-solving task will be even greater if that child is from another country, has a different language, or does not share the same hearing status. In both of these problem-solving "tasks," children apply what they know to novel situations in order to achieve some goal. The extent to which this application of prior knowledge and skills happens automatically (with or without thinking about it) reflects the cognitive (or social or linguistic) flexibility of the child. As such, it says something about what they know, how that knowledge is organized, and how they use that knowledge—all part of the *metacognitive* and *executive function* abilities discussed earlier. Let's take a look at some of these issues.

EXPERIENCE AND CONCEPTUAL DEVELOPMENT

Exposure to a variety of experiences and environments is an essential part of children's development, both their hardware (brain) and software (knowledge and strategies). Studies involving rats have shown that when they are raised alone in a cage with no "toys" or other kinds of stimulation, their brain cells (*neurons*) remain rather simple, with few branchings (see Figure 8.1). Rats raised with fellow rats, running wheels, and other "stimulating" objects have brain cells that have many more branchings and interconnections. More complex brain structure and greater interconnections among brain cells are indicators of greater intelligence and cognitive flexibility across species as well as across individuals of the same species. We do not have to open up deaf children's brains to know that those who have had more varied experiences with the environment, people, things, and language will be more flexible and likely have better academic outcomes than children with less experience.

Deaf children who are unable to communicate effectively with family members or who are overprotected by well-meaning adults likely will have fewer "interesting" interactions with the world and less diversity in their experiences compared to either hearing children or deaf children who have full access to the language

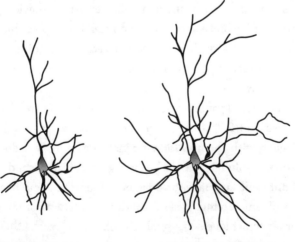

Individual cage   Complex environment

FIGURE 8.1 Photographs of brain cells show more branches and interconnections as a result of more diverse experience during development. (Courtesy W. T. Greenough)

of those around them. That is one reason why deaf children of deaf parents and deaf children with cochlear implants, *on average*, have advantages over deaf children without those benefits. In neither case do they usually have quite as much access or quite as much diversity as hearing children of the same age, but probably there is no *threshold* or lower limit for how much such experience is necessary for "normal" development. Even among hearing children, there is wide variability in these areas, and we sometimes see that reflected in differences between children of lower and higher socioeconomic status, rural versus urban children, and children in developed versus developing countries. But we also see that children are very resilient, and normal development can occur in very abnormal environments.

Putting such theoretical issues aside, even when deaf and hearing children are in the same environment, they may have different experiences (just as twins do). Those differences are not only a consequence of having more or less hearing but also of their language fluencies and even the mode(s) of their language (sign and/or speech). These differences all subsequently affect the kinds of people and situations with which children have interactions. They also may have differing access to formal and informal education, so that they learn different things at different times and in different ways. Some of these differences will prove to be positive. For example, as we saw in Chapter 7, deaf children are more likely than hearing children to rely on visual memory, a strategy that results in their having better memory for locations and faces.

Other differences may prove to have a negative influence on learning. As we will see later, for example, deaf children too often focus on only one aspect of a task that requires looking at the bigger picture of a task and how the parts fit together—like trying to win in *Monopoly* rather than just moving around the board. Why they behave this way is still unclear. It could be related to deaf children's depending on one sense (sight) rather than being experienced in integrating information from two senses (sight and hearing). It also may result from the willingness of teachers to accept simple, one-dimensional answers from deaf students rather than encouraging deeper, more extended discussions about things. All too often, deaf students are allowed to get by with less than would be required of hearing students, thus depriving them of valuable educational experiences. If you set lower expectations, children's outcomes usually will match them.

In a later section of this chapter, we will consider how language acquisition and cognitive development are both facilitated by experiences that show children the links between concepts and their labels. Children are able to construct this simple primitive conceptual system in part because the language and behaviors of adults (and older children) divide up the world in ways that make cognitive, social, and cultural sense. A child thus can go about language acquisition and concept learning as problem-solving tasks, implicitly or explicitly noting relations and underlying rules while filtering out irrelevant information. This active learning requires a range of experience—the more you have, the better off you're going to be. Restrictions on deaf children's experiences, therefore, may have broad implications for development and learning.

Research involving hearing children has shown that vocabulary development is positively related to the time spent with different adults in diverse settings. The frequency of informal, everyday language interactions between parents and children is the best predictor of language development, and by age 3, at least 95% of a child's vocabulary has come from his parents. Vocabulary development also is greater in children who have mothers who are less controlling and provide more opportunities for exploration. Similar studies have not been conducted involving deaf children, but these same results would be expected as long as the relevant adults are able to communicate effectively with the children.

INTEGRATION AND ORGANIZATION OF KNOWLEDGE

If you ask a group of hearing high school students to give you the first word that comes to mind when you say the word "dog," almost all of them will say "cat." If the same question is put to a group of deaf students, a majority may still say "cat," but there will also be a variety of other answers including "food," "show," and "Frisky," many given by only a single individual. Studies using such methods have revealed several differences in how deaf and hearing students' knowledge is organized. Most obviously from this example, a classroom full of hearing students will have more similar knowledge compared to a comparably sized class of deaf students.

Studies also have shown that the strength of the connections between concepts (like "cat" and "dog" or "animal" and "living") generally are not as strong for deaf students as they are for hearing students. Partly as a result, deaf students are more likely than hearing students to read one word at a time, because words in a sentence are less likely to mentally activate other words that are likely to follow. Similarly, deaf students are less likely to make connections among phrases in sentences or sentences in a printed passage. In essence, they do not automatically "predict" the meaning of what they are reading. From our own research, we suspect that something similar happens in their comprehension of sign language or speech, but those studies have not been done. In any case, the weaker connections among concepts not only will affect language comprehension but also will affect problem solving and learning more generally. A deaf student, for example, may be less likely than hearing classmates to make the connection between friction and the heat generated by tires on a road.

So why do we find this difference in knowledge organization? As suggested previously, it's all about experience. The more times that two things are experienced together, the stronger will be their connection (*association*). That connection does not have to be experienced "in person," but it also can occur through language (think about "sun" and "moon" as opposed to "paper" and "book") or even in your own head. Other than in intentional learning, as in learning something for school, how well something is retained depends on how often it is experienced either directly or indirectly.

An example of direct, or explicit learning might be the learning of a nursery rhyme, particularly one that a child might learn without understanding the words (e.g., *Mares eat oats and does eat oats, but little lambs eat ivy*). An example of indirect learning of associations might be children's understanding of categories and their members. The fact that a cow is an animal might be learned directly, but that it is a member of the category of four-legged animals, the category of farm animals, and the category of not very bright animals typically will be inferred or learned incidentally. But let us put the associations between categories and their members into two larger cognitive contexts, one relating to the use of category knowledge and the more general process of using such knowledge during problem solving and learning.

Concepts and Categories

There was a memory study some years ago in which the researcher asked deaf elementary school children to sort a set of pictures into piles that "went together." In response, the children made piles corresponding to categories (animals, clothing), indicating that they "had" those categories. After the cards had been removed, however, and the children were asked to name all of the pictures they had seen, the children did not repeat back the pictures according to those categories, as hearing children do. In other words, although the children understood the categories, they did not use their category knowledge in the memory (problem-solving) task. This result was interpreted as indicating that the deaf children either have lesser category knowledge or that their category knowledge is less stable than it is for hearing children. Based on studies that we have conducted since, it appears more likely that the deaf children did not recognize the usefulness of a category-based memory retrieval strategy, making the aforementioned finding more a function of metacognition and executive functioning (see Chapter 6) rather than related to category knowledge per se.

Before we look at how deaf children deal with multiple aspects of problems or multiple dimensions of objects or concepts, it is worth noting that the differing likelihood of concepts connecting to each other (in memory) can have real consequences for the academic outcomes of deaf and hearing children. Experienced teachers of deaf children recognize that, on average, their students have vocabulary and conceptual knowledge somewhat less rich and more variable across children than is the case for hearing children. The rates at which they learn new words and meanings also are slower. Several researchers have suggested that this finding may be the result of deaf children's relatively limited vocabulary knowledge not being very helpful in acquiring new vocabulary. Certainly there does not appear to be any difficulty associated with learning new words when appropriate experience (and accommodation for visual attention) is provided.

Regardless of their origins, these findings suggest that many deaf learners are at risk in settings where new information is structured for hearing learners by instructors who are unfamiliar with differences between deaf and hearing students' knowledge. Skilled teachers of the deaf use two instructional strategies to deal with this issue, both of which appear likely to support deaf students' learning while providing their teachers with important feedback regarding their students' readiness for greater breadth and depth of instruction. One approach involves the use of concept maps and other diagrams to depict relations among various concepts and the possibility of their being members of different categories at the same time. The second is the use of games or other activities aimed at demonstrating similarities and differences among concepts at different levels, including lexical (name), perceptual (color), practical (use), categorical, and so on.

These strategies are often used with younger children, both deaf and hearing. However, research findings indicating that deaf children and even college-age deaf students frequently fail to use category, functional, and perceptual knowledge in problem solving suggests that related methods might need to be used with deaf students who are older than would be expected on the basis of findings from hearing students. Studies involving experienced teachers of deaf children and young adults have shown success in using such methods, but the possibility of transfer of such training across tasks (*generalization*), their effects on metacognition, and their long-term impact on learning have not been evaluated. Simply providing such supporting materials before or during learning does not improve performance for either deaf or hearing students, however, unless those materials are actively used by the student to process the new information. The challenge, therefore, is to find a way to have deaf students take in such information and use it spontaneously to support their understanding and learning (see Box 8.1).

BOX 8.1
USING CATEGORY KNOWLEDGE IN READING

Research with college students has revealed an interesting asymmetry in deaf students' category knowledge. For hearing students, categories and their most strongly associated members, like "animal" and "dog," are symmetrically related, so that the connection from each to the other is about the same. For deaf students, in contrast, "dog" is more strongly related to "animal" than "animal" is to "dog." In terms of the real world rather than laboratory performance, that means that when hearing children hear or read a sentence beginning with "The dog ran . . ." or "The animal ran . . ." the fact that a dog is an animal is equally likely to be activated and available to help with comprehension (running somewhere or in some way, different from water or paint running). In the case of "The animal ran . . .," other commonly encountered animals that run (cats and horses, but not birds) also will be activated in long-term memory, perhaps along with other relevant knowledge. Deaf children reading, hearing, or seeing a signed sentence beginning with "The animal ran . . ." are less likely to activate the dog knowledge than they are to activate animal knowledge when they encounter a sentence beginning with "The dog ran . . ." As a result, comprehension of the sentence will be slower and perhaps less rich (for example, there may not be an accompanying visual image). This finding is related to the tendency of many deaf children to approach problems in relatively concrete terms, attending to one aspect of a situation or task at a time.

Integration of Information

The category memory study described in the previous section not only told us something about deaf children's knowledge of concepts and categories, it also demonstrated what is now a frequent finding: that deaf students often fail to apply knowledge that we know they have or is made available to them in the context of classroom or problem-solving tasks. For example, we have known for decades that deaf and hearing children perform similarly when memory, problem-solving, and learning tasks involve only a single dimension. Sorting cards from the *SET* game on shape, number, or color, for instance, would look essentially the same in deaf and hearing children. When correct responses require the integration or balancing of multiple dimensions, however, like sorting *SET* cards according to number *and* color at the same time, deaf children usually perform at levels below hearing age-mates.

The results from studies of deaf students' problem solving are similar to those from studies of their reading. For example, one indicator that deaf students are reading one word at a time is the finding that they often tend to remember material as disconnected words or phrases. Hearing children, in contrast, tend to remember meaningful chunks of what they read. Such evidence highlights the need for teachers of deaf students to provide a richer context for instruction than they normally would for hearing students, explicitly tying new information to what students already know rather than depending on them to make appropriate inferences.

Ultimately, of course, the goal is to have deaf children make inferences for themselves when they read, when they attend to a teacher or someone else, or when they are solving a problem. Inference making, however, depends on recognizing the usefulness of what is already known and integrating that knowledge with new information, both areas in which deaf students tend to lag behind hearing peers. Parents and teachers therefore need to be wary of always providing explicit connections between ideas (the *controlling* tendency we mentioned earlier); rather, it is important that they teach deaf children how to do this themselves. Because of the greater variability in their concept knowledge and their lesser likelihood of automatically retrieving relevant information from memory, teachers also need to ensure that students recognize the importance of such *relational processing* and that the new information is understood, processed, and retained.

FINAL WORDS

In this chapter, we have seen differences between deaf and hearing children in what they know and how they use what they know. Such differences result, in part, from issues of cognition, learning, and memory that were discussed in the previous two chapters. At the same time, they also are affected by language and social interactions that had their origins much earlier. We therefore can see that learning is cumulative and interactive, a description we offered in Chapter 2 (see Figure 2.1). As children get older and experience learning in the formal setting of the classroom, earlier knowledge and skills come to bear in helping them acquire even more. With their constant growth in cognitive complexity and flexibility, children are increasingly ready to take on new kinds of learning in new kinds of situations.

An important aspect of learning, both in school and out of school, involves the transfer of knowledge and skills from one context to another. Being able to draw on previous knowledge and experience (memory) and apply it to new situations (problem solving) is essential to academic success as well as social and language growth. The fact that deaf and hearing children have different knowledge is not surprising given their different experiences and the different ways that they take in information from the environment. The fact that such differences affect their brains as well as their behavior also is not surprising. It is only through being aware of all this that we can modify instructional materials and methods in order to offer deaf children the best opportunities for learning. At this point, however, all of the basic building blocks of learning are in place, and we are ready to see how the blocks are assembled for higher level tasks such as reading and mathematics.

9

READING

THE READING SKILLS of deaf students have perhaps been the most discussed and studied topic among educators and researchers interested in deaf education. The near obsession with reading comes from the consistent finding that deaf students, on average, do not read as well as their hearing peers, and yet reading is essential for their schooling, eventual employment, and quality of life. Many hearing children also have difficulty reading at the levels expected by their state education standards. Among deaf children, however, reading comprehension below grade level is the rule rather than the exception. Later, we will describe results from researchers who have studied deaf students who read (and write) particularly well. Meanwhile, we will examine "why Johnny can't read" and what we can do about it.

We should admit going into this topic that the solution(s) to this centuries-old problem are still unclear, but we can shed some light on what we do know, what we don't know, and what we think we know. We also note in advance that we believe that we know more than we think we do. That is, research evidence concerning the cognitive and language development of deaf children, as well as recent work on classroom learning, lead us to some good ideas about the challenge of reading for deaf children and why we have not been more successful in improving it. With all of the different beliefs in the field concerning deaf children's reading, however, translating that research into practical teaching and learning strategies will be another matter.

THE CHALLENGE OF LEARNING TO READ

Researchers have addressed the question of why deaf students have so much trouble reading from different angles. One approach is related to how deaf students process written information in the absence of sound-based information when they read. In essence, this is the question of whether deaf students have *phonological awareness* of printed words: How can someone read if he cannot effectively "sound out" words in his head? This is a cognitive skill assumed by many reading experts to be necessary for children to develop successful reading skills.

Do Deaf Children Have Phonological Awareness?

Many readers will be familiar with *phonics*, what we normally think of as being able to figure out new words by "sounding them out." Phonics and *phonemic awareness*—the ability to recognize differences among the sounds of written and spoken language—together are generally referred to as *phonological awareness*. Most educators and researchers assume that phonological awareness is necessary for reading. But can you recognize and use letter sounds if you can't hear?

Skilled deaf and hard-of-hearing readers do appear to use phonological information during reading in order to link printed words to their meanings. But it is not clear that they use this phonological information much in learning to read. While it is true that such knowledge is most easily acquired through hearing and speaking, there is evidence that some deaf children create similar codes in working memory by integrating information obtained through a combination of signing, fingerspelling, *orthography* (the way words look), articulation, speechreading, and any remaining hearing. But it is not clear which children learn to do that or how they do it.

Children who receive cochlear implants early pronounce letter sounds more accurately than do children with the same levels of hearing loss who benefit from hearing aids, and they also read better, even if they still lag behind hearing children. Systems like cued speech and Visual Phonics (see Chapter 4) appear to improve phonological processing among some deaf children, but not well enough to have them reading at grade level. Most deaf readers thus have only limited knowledge of phonology during the early school years, and they sometimes fail to apply that knowledge when it is available. Instead, they rely more on how printed words look, the *orthography*, even when spelling does not match the way words sound (e.g., *cave*, *have*).

Studies of the development of language and literacy in deaf individuals have found that phonological awareness is not a good predictor of reading ability in deaf children even if it is in hearing children. Some investigators have suggested that phonological awareness might actually be a result of learning to read rather than or in addition to the other way around, particularly for deaf children. This is another example of the interactive, cumulative nature of learning and ways that deaf and hearing children differ.

Hearing children who are not successful in learning phonics sometimes are taught to become *sight readers*, learning to recognize words as visual wholes instead of by their individual parts or letter-sound correspondences. Skilled readers sight read familiar words, recognizing words on the page without having to sound out each one, even if they originally learned to read through phonics. Judging by the kinds of errors that deaf students make in their spelling (e.g., *ornge*, *decihper*), it appears that many of them are sight readers as well. For both them and hearing readers without phonics, however, encountering printed words that are unfamiliar creates problems, because they are unable to determine whether they know the meaning based on how it sounds.

How Does First Language Fluency Affect Reading?

If you look at the scientific research concerning deaf children's first language and their reading abilities, there is a fascinating situation that, unfortunately, demonstrates the history of educational philosophies being given more credibility than hard evidence. People who support "oral" education for deaf children point out that studies have shown a strong relationship between children's spoken language skills and their reading ability. People who support sign language in the education of deaf children point out that studies have shown a strong relationship between deaf children's sign language skills and their reading ability. Who is right? Actually, both are. The research tells us that children who have strong skills in their first language are better readers, regardless of whether they are deaf or hearing, and regardless of whether they are learning sign language or spoken language. As we suggested earlier, some of the skills associated with fluent reading are acquired or improved through reading, and they do not have to be fully developed prior to learning to read. In Chapter 10, we will see that the same is true of the skills that make up children's mathematics abilities.

These findings emphasize that having a strong language background is part of *school readiness* and an essential component of learning to read, in particular. Many of the basics of reading also are acquired before entering school: which way to hold a book, that there is a correspondence between talking and words on the page, and that each word on a page has meaning. Even when deaf children have mastered some of the prereading skills, however, the transition to the reading itself is frequently difficult at least in part because they are often learning to read while they are still learning their first language.

Importantly in this regard, we have known for a long time that language acquisition has a *critical period*, or at least a *sensitive period*, in which it is easier to learn language. Between birth and age 3, children's brains are like sponges, able to learn languages faster and more easily than they can at later ages (as most of us know from our own school years). Having to learn a first language later not only has consequences for (slower and less fluent) language learning but also has cognitive and academic consequences. This situation is frequently seen in deaf children whose parents first tried to have them learn spoken language and only later, at age 5 or 7, "give up" and let them acquire sign language. Already lagging behind in their knowledge of the world and in various cognitive processes, it is not only the late learning of language that is going to create difficulties. Deaf children who acquire their first language before the age of 3 will perform differently on language and cognitive tasks than will children who do so after age 3, just as would be the case for hearing children.

Knowledge, Vocabulary, and Reading

In Chapter 8, we saw that the organization of knowledge in long-term memory is somewhat different between deaf and hearing individuals, due in part to their differing experiences and access to language growing up. During reading, we rely on previous knowledge relating to the concepts and content of what we are reading to support comprehension. This is referred to as *top-down processing*, and it clearly is affected by what and how much we know as well as perhaps to the organization of the knowledge (and how easy it is to get out of memory). Top-down processing is contrasted with *bottom-up processing*, or taking information from the printed page and adding it to what we know (in memory). It should be apparent that top-down and bottom-up processing take place all the time during reading as well as in "through-the-air" communication, although it is not as often discussed in this context.

The interaction of top-down and bottom-up processing means that what we know about the meanings of individual words and how they go together allows us to understand the words and sentences on the printed page (or the sounds or signs that reach our ears and eyes), at the same time as those words and sentences make contact with what we already know. In this paragraph, for example, there are no new words, but there are new ideas expressed through words you already know. If you didn't know the meanings of the words, didn't have the prior knowledge gained from earlier chapters of this book and your own experience and schooling, this paragraph would make no more sense than if you were reading a foreign language. You could still "read" the words and sentences, just like people can read Lewis Carroll's *Jabberwocky*, but you would not be comprehending. That is exactly what happens to the deaf child who does not have the knowledge or language to support age-appropriate reading.

Although we have been talking about *knowledge* in the previous paragraphs, it should be mentioned that knowledge as it relates to reading is closely linked to *vocabulary*. Knowledge may not be very helpful for reading if we do not have the words or signs to communicate it or to acquire it. It therefore will not be surprising that how many words children know (*vocabulary size*) is strongly related to how well they read. Actually, the relationship works in both directions: Having larger vocabularies helps children learn to read, and reading helps to build larger vocabularies. Vocabulary size among deaf children, however, typically is smaller than among hearing children, creating barriers to reading and writing that could otherwise enhance further language development, vocabulary growth, reading, and so on.

Deaf children's smaller vocabularies likely result from multiple causes, including limitations on their incidental learning and insufficient top-down processing strategies to be able to take advantage of whatever language they can access. Parents and other adults also may use more limited vocabularies in interactions with deaf children, sometimes due to lowered expectations concerning a child's knowledge and language ability and sometimes due to the adults' own lack of communication skill.

Recent research has found that deaf children's learning of written vocabulary is easier when they already know signs for the concepts. When a printed word is encountered over and over, understanding of its meaning and its connections to related concepts becomes stronger (see Chapter 8). This process makes the understanding of sentences easier through top-down processing, supporting children's acquisition of the grammar (or *syntax*) of the language as well as new knowledge. In this way, vocabulary learning and grammar support each other in learning to read. In addition, this kind of interaction reduces the amount of effort necessary for working memory (see Chapter 7), making reading easier and more pleasurable.

WHAT CAN WE DO ABOUT DEAF STUDENTS' READING ACHIEVEMENT?

We wish we could write a couple of paragraphs explaining exactly what we can do to improve deaf students' reading achievement. Unfortunately, we can't. We know that there are successful deaf readers from different educational and family backgrounds who use different forms of communication. We know that access to language at home and at school is key, and that children who have a fluent first language learn to read faster and easier than those who do not. Cochlear implants lead to better reading abilities for many deaf children, but the fact that they still lag behind hearing peers indicates that there is more to reading than hearing. Also consistent with this suggestion are recent research findings indicating that students with implants who were reading at grade level at 8 to 9 years of age have significantly more trouble by the time they reach high school.

There are some things we can do to help deaf children learn to read and to read better. One of these is *shared reading*. Shared reading means just that: sharing the activity of reading with a child. The story in a book first might be "told" without regard for the actual text, just by looking at and pointing to the pictures. We can then read it (spoken or signed), occasionally stopping to ask the child questions or link the text to the pictures. Parents can point out associations between printed words and either spoken words or signs. These activities introduce children to the idea of reading and can make reading a pleasurable experience. Shared reading works better when parents follow the child's lead in deciding the focus of attention and how long they spend with a book.

Shared reading occurs often in many families, but rarely if at all in others. Hearing parents of deaf children often hesitate to "read" with them, assuming that because their communication is not very smooth, it will not be useful. Other parents assume that their deaf children will not enjoy books, and they are unsure how to create interest and sustain attention with them. With the right books (that have the right pictures), however, most children, deaf or hearing, will find them interesting and will enjoy shared reading.

We should point out, however, that the benefits of shared reading for deaf children fit into the category of "what we think we know." Studies involving hearing children have shown that shared reading during the preschool and elementary school years leads to better reading comprehension. Although shared reading is frequently advocated for deaf children, there do not appear to have been any controlled studies evaluating its helpfulness. Shared reading can't do any harm, however, and even if it does not lead to specific advantages in reading, it will be another opportunity for language and social interactions between parents and their deaf child.

Another activity that is likely to support deaf children's recognition and comprehension of words involves increasing the number of senses through which children experience word meanings (hearing, seeing, smelling, touching). Consistent with our earlier descriptions of learning and memory, where having both verbal and nonverbal mental representations of concepts was better than either alone, providing children with multiple sensory experiences increases the speed of learning and memorability of new words. Preliminary studies have found that this approach is more effective than learning words through language alone, but hearing children benefitted more than deaf children, presumably because they had more knowledge and language (that is, top-down processing) to support further learning.

Time on task definitely is as important for reading as it is for other kinds of learning. Parents and teachers have long known that children who read better read more. What was not clear was whether they read more because they were better readers or that reading more made them better readers. Research has now shown that the second scenario is the case. True, children who read better are likely to find reading more fun and therefore do it more, but reading more does improve reading, which makes it more pleasurable, leading to more reading, and so on.

Some educators and researchers seeking to improve deaf children's reading ability have developed a variety of simplified reading materials, sometimes called *basal readers*. The assumption was that *natural texts* (just regular books) often are too difficult for deaf children, who lack the basic skills necessary to understand them. In general, however, research has not shown that basal readers are effective. As we saw earlier with regard to beginning readers, children do not need to have in place all of the skills necessary for reading more complex materials before they begin to try. Consistent with what we know about other areas of child development, a moderate amount of difficulty plus expectations for success help children to grow, moving to "the next level." Giving them simplified materials does not encourage such growth.

One difficulty that arises with deaf children who are not reading at age-appropriate levels is that the books they can read often have content better suited to younger children, while books that would be of interest to them really are too difficult. In this situation, comic books and magazines can be helpful, because they usually are written at a lower level than books intended for children of the same age. There is no evidence, however, to support claims that television captions, texting, and the Internet improve deaf students' reading. This makes sense because all three usually involve ungrammatical and nonstandard language.

At this point, let us come back to the studies we mentioned earlier and consider those deaf students who are the best readers. How did they get that way? From the previous discussion, it can be correctly assumed that children who have better language skills and read more become better readers. More specifically, studies have looked at the best deaf readers to try to discover what it was in their backgrounds that led them to the top. Notice that this is different from examining relationships between reading and language, time on task, or other factors, which involves looking at students with a wide range of reading abilities.

When we look at only the best deaf readers, we find that there is essentially one factor that separates them from all of the others: the amount of parent involvement in their child's education. Those parents who are most involved will be the ones who learn to communicate effectively with their deaf child, engage in reading-related activities, help with homework, ensure that their child has a wide range of experience with people and things, and participate in their child's school activities, both academic and nonacademic. Importantly, it doesn't matter whether those parents are deaf or hearing.

Parents and teachers often will benefit from obtaining strategies for reading intervention from teachers who have successfully taught deaf children how to read. As in other areas of development, the methods for teaching deaf children to read, especially at the level of grammar and understanding larger amounts of text, will be different in some ways than methods used with hearing children. Strategies for working with visual learners, with children who may be lagging in their language skills, and children with knowledge somewhat different than hearing children will not always be obvious.

Notice that we said a good resource would be "teachers who have successfully taught deaf children how to read." Some companies advertise reading programs, say that they can teach deaf children to read, and claim to know the true path. Most of these interventions lack any evidence of their effectiveness, and even if they work with some deaf children, they may not work with many others. It therefore is important for parents and teachers to do their homework before adopting a reading program; they should look into whether it has been successful with deaf children, not just with hearing children, and whether there are achievement data to back up their claims. Some of this information can be found on the Internet (Has the program been used successfully with deaf students?), but better sources are other parents of deaf children, university teacher-of-the-deaf training programs, and organizations that support deaf children and their families.

A FEW WORDS ABOUT WRITING

Because reading and writing are so closely related, it should not be surprising that the level of deaf children's performance in one usually is similar to their level in the other. For example, deaf children tend to write using shorter sentences than hearing peers and to repeatedly use simple subject-verb-object sentences. This often gives the appearance of writing by much younger children. Deaf children also frequently leave out words when they write, particularly adverbs, conjunctions, and auxiliary verbs, while the frequencies of using nouns and verbs is about the same. The resulting choppy pattern could result from either deaf children trying to "write in signed language" when they do not have sufficient sign fluency to recognize signed adverbs, conjunctions, and auxiliary verbs or the fact that those words are unstressed in speech and thus are likely to be missed by students with lesser hearing sensitivity (or both). Meanwhile, studies of deaf students' writing have shown that it can be rich and creative, even if it suffers in ways that many mothers and English teachers might find unacceptable. Such writing indicates that deaf children have partial understanding of the rules of writing but frequently lack the vocabulary and grammatical tools to express their thoughts "correctly."

Studies of deaf students' writing not only look at how well they write. Educators who have looked at deaf students' writing in the classroom have recommended using writing activities to teach science or other subjects to deaf and hard-of-hearing students. Students can participate in concrete, hands-on activities in the classroom and then write about what they learned. Rather than focusing on the quality of the English in students' writing (although you can do that, too), such activities give students practice in integrating ideas, explaining relationships, and identifying the important points in what they have learned. In guiding students' thinking and encouraging active evaluation of their own knowledge, writing can help students to exercise the cognitive and metacognitive skills that they need for successful learning. At the same time, having something interesting to write about without being overly concerned about grammar and punctuation gives students motivation to write more. Similar projects have involved encouraging deaf and hard-of-hearing students to keep journals and share them with parents or teachers who can give them feedback (not criticism!) about their ideas and help them reflect on their own writing. As with writing in class, such activities can help improve students' writing and their interest in writing while supporting cognitive skills needed for academic success.

FINAL WORDS

Much more research is needed on how to best teach deaf children how to read and write. The lack of progress in this regard over the past hundred years is disappointing, but recent studies have at least pointed us in the right direction. Some reading instruction programs—like some language programs—appear to be beneficial, even if they have not yet yielded any evidence of their success. With the current emphasis on *evidence-based practice* in schools (instructional methods that research has shown to be successful), it is not enough to claim that a program works; its effectiveness needs to be demonstrated. Toward this end, school and program interventions that appear to work for deaf children need to allow their methods to be studied. In particular, we need to observe and analyze the methods and materials used in classrooms that have been found to produce comparable learning by deaf and hearing students. We need to figure out in what settings those methods can be successful, with which students, and at what ages. We know there are teachers who work closely with their deaf students and who intuitively "know" how to teach them to read. In some cases, those intuitions turn out to be correct, and in others they don't. Teachers may not always realize what it is that they are doing right, just as they may not recognize other things they do that either create barriers to deaf children's learning or have no real effect. It is time that research and practice in deaf education move closer together, bringing research into the classroom and encouraging teachers to lead the way in raising research questions.

DOING MATH

Foundations and Outcomes

AFTER READING, MOST of the research concerning deaf children's academic achievement and most efforts at intervention have involved mathematics. In part, this focus follows from the standards and testing procedures of most school systems. But mathematics is also of special importance in education—particularly for deaf children—because of the reasoning and problem-solving skills it requires and which it later helps to support. Like reading, grasp of mathematics will have a long-term impact on deaf children's educational attainments and, eventually, on their employment opportunities. Unfortunately, as with literacy, deaf children frequently lag behind hearing peers in their mathematical skills and their understanding of number and magnitude (*quantitative*) concepts, even before they enter school. Partly as a result, during the school years, deaf students' mathematics achievement scores are only about 80% of those attained by hearing students, a situation that has not changed much over the past 30 years.

The primary reasons for this situation appear to be *(1)* a relative lack of early experiences with quantitative concepts, *(2)* delays in language development, *(3)* insufficient teaching credentials and instructional practices by those who teach mathematics to deaf children, and *(4)* sensory- and language-based differences in the ways that deaf and hearing children process information. All of these, of course, are related to the experiential, cognitive, and teaching issues we have discussed in the previous chapters.

So let us take a closer look at how they relate to deaf children's learning and achievement in mathematics.

UNDERSTANDING NUMBER

Research involving hearing infants has indicated that even before they begin learning language, they recognize differences in number or quantity (see Box 10.1). This finding suggests some innate basis for the learning of mathematics and emphasizes the importance of ensuring that young children are exposed to number concepts and the thinking normally associated with it. Consistent with the importance of early experience—and with the first two explanations for mathematics underachievement mentioned earlier—recent studies have found that preschool-aged deaf children with at least one deaf parent who uses sign language have better quantitative skills than those with hearing parents.

That research has shown that deaf parents more frequently refer to mathematical concepts (*more, all, everything, some*) and are more likely to expose their children to number concepts than other parents. Once again, high parental expectations are also important, because deaf children showing more age-appropriate mathematical skills were those who were exposed to more problem-solving situations where number or quantity was relevant.

The language issue is also relevant in the classroom, simply because interactions can be more spontaneous and focused when teachers and students can communicate fluently with each other. But there must be more involved in young deaf

BOX 10.1

HOW CAN WE KNOW WHETHER BABIES UNDERSTAND NUMBER?

Research aimed at finding out what babies know often uses what is called the *habituation paradigm*. The idea is that babies will look at something that is new and "interesting" longer than something that is old and "boring." Thus, if you show an infant a picture of three identical clowns, at first she will spend time looking at them but gradually will pay less and less attention (*habituation*). If you add a fourth clown and she still mostly ignores the picture, it indicates that she does not recognize that the quantities "three" and "four" are different. If she starts paying attention again when the fourth clown is added, it indicates that she does have some understanding that the three clowns and the four clowns are different. That is, she understands that "three" and "four" are different quantities.

children's acquiring number knowledge than just early access to language, because the highest-scoring children with deaf parents tend to score only at the "average" level for hearing children. Then again, at least 95% of deaf parents had hearing parents themselves, and as youngsters they may not have gained strong foundations in either language or mathematics from parent–child communication. As parents themselves, they still might lack full competence in those domains, perhaps passing on struggles to their own children.[1] Evaluation of this possibility would require studies of multigeneration deaf families, research that has not yet been conducted. Another possibility, consistent with discussions in earlier chapters, is that deaf children require somewhat different experiences than hearing children to give them the essentials of mathematical understanding, and we have not yet fully identified what these experiences should look like. Finally, we should emphasize again that parents have to *expect* that their deaf children will succeed in mathematics and other subjects. Asian American children, who frequently excel at mathematics and science, do not have any innate abilities different from their peers. What they do have are parents and families that value hard work and success in such fields—and have high expectations for their children.

Following up on the discussion of memory in Chapter 7, delays in preschoolers' number competencies often appear greatest in language-based, sequential tasks such as counting or producing number sequences by *rote* (from memory, not counting actual things). At the same time, deaf preschoolers are able to reproduce the number of objects presented to them one at a time, by placing the same number of chips in front of them. Deaf children do better than hearing peers in such tasks when the objects are presented in a spatial array, consistent with what we know about their visual processing skills. Findings like these show that young deaf children understand some important basic number concepts, even if they frequently are delayed in making number comparisons (*more* and *less*), counting by numbers other than one (e.g., 2, 4, 6...), and in reading and writing multidigit numbers (e.g., 475, 5482). Thus, the foundations of their mathematical learning are uneven when they enter school, putting them at risk of falling farther behind when formal mathematical instruction begins. It is therefore important for parents to engage their young deaf children in games and other activities that involve number, size and quantity comparisons, and fractions. Baking cookies (e.g., *This tray is bigger,* or *How many can we fit on this one?*), artwork (e.g., *Let's make four small ones instead of one big one*), and just informal talk about things (e.g., *Look at that window . . . it has four pieces of glass*) in the environment all can work and should not be underestimated. At the same time, this will help to strengthen the emotional bond between parents and children.

UNDERSTANDING MATHEMATICS DURING THE SCHOOL YEARS

The lag between deaf and hearing children in their understanding of mathematics operations and number concepts generally continues and even becomes larger during the school years. The extent to which this is the result of having poorer foundational skills or a consequence of the way they are taught is unclear. Either way, because they came to school with different cognitive and number-related skills, they likely would benefit from somewhat different materials and methodologies in mathematics instruction. Several studies have indicated that the mathematical and problem-solving experiences usually provided to deaf children in school are not enough for them to attain age-appropriate academic levels.

The (U.S.) National Council of Teachers of Mathematics recommends frequent problem-solving work in the classroom for all children, particularly with *story problems* (those based on real-world use of mathematics). Several researchers have argued for the need to provide even more practice with word problems for deaf children, but they usually get less of it than hearing children. Surveys have shown that teachers who had at least one mathematics methods course ("how to teach math") during their teacher training use story problems more frequently than those who did not. That experience not only provides teachers with a better understanding of mathematical concepts and how to teach them, but it gives them more confidence in communicating the subject matter, something likely to be of great importance when they are unsure of their abilities in teaching deaf children or others with special needs.

Regrettably, studies have also found that many teachers believe that story problems, whether presented "through the air" or in written form, are too difficult for deaf children until they have mastered basic math skills. As a result, regardless of whether they teach in separate programs for deaf children, mainstream classes with both deaf and hearing children, or special deaf classes within mainstream schools, most teachers emphasize visual problem-solving strategies for deaf students— using diagrams, illustrations, signing, and hands-on activities—rather than more analytically oriented strategies that would be of greater and more general utility. Having already come into school behind in their mathematical skills, deaf children's experience thus continues to be limited during the school years.

Please do not misunderstand us here. Visual materials can be extremely helpful in relating mathematical problems to the real world and showing relations between a problem and its component parts. They do have an important place in the classroom. Yet research has shown that many deaf students who use visual materials frequently do not do so effectively, often failing to get the right answer to problems even with those supports. Instead of trying to make problems more concrete, a better approach would be to use story problems and similar tasks to help build the skills that those children are missing. Teachers can describe the importance of identifying the goals and key pieces of information in a problem and the separate operations required to solve it. In the process, they can demonstrate estimation, planning, and evaluation of results (*modeling*). In this way, they can show the difference between a trial-and-error approach to problem solving and the more efficient method of making and testing of hypotheses. Breaking down problems into their parts (*analytic* problem solving) will help to encourage the relational processing and metacognition we discussed in Chapters 6 and 8. To paraphrase an old saying, the goal should be not to give the child a fish, but to teach him how to solve the problem of fishing.

While the *amount* of time that teachers of the deaf spend on problem-solving activities does not appear to differ depending on where they teach, there are some instructional differences across settings. For example, grade-appropriate math textbooks are more likely to be used in regular school classrooms than in separate classrooms for deaf children either within mainstream programs or in separate programs for deaf children. Teachers in regular school classrooms also tend to be better qualified to teach mathematics and more likely to have backgrounds in math. Not surprisingly, perhaps, those teachers who are certified in mathematics education are more likely than the others to encourage children to use analytic problem-solving strategies, including the use of analogies to understand word problems and relate them to what children already know. These are skills that all children need and can use in other subjects as well. We saw in Chapter 8, however, that deaf children often lack these skills.

Do you think you have noticed a contradiction? We have mentioned several times that experienced teachers of the deaf are more aware of deaf students' strengths and needs and therefore are able to adjust their teaching accordingly. Yet here we have suggested that teachers in mainstream classrooms are more likely to give deaf students important experience with challenging and flexible approaches to problem solving and to have high expectations for those students. This is not really a contradiction but an example of the difference between "what we think" and "what we know." Many teachers of the deaf think that an emphasis on visual materials is the way to teach deaf children mathematics, and as a result some deaf students never gain the analytic problem-solving skills important for mathematics and other subjects. Teachers in mainstream classrooms may not be as sensitive to deaf students' needs as visual learners, but being more likely to have training in mathematics, they typically are more aware of what it is that children need to succeed in math. Fortunately, there are classrooms in which all of this comes together.

If deaf children end up with better mathematics skills, a large part of that success thus can be attributed to the training, background, and appropriate instructional strategies of their teachers.

Speaking of expectations, although there is little research on the topic, it appears that teachers' perceptions and expectations for deaf students also vary across school settings. These, too, affect academic outcomes. Studies have shown that mathematics teachers working with deaf students in regular classrooms tend to have more positive perceptions of their students' problem-solving abilities and higher expectations than teachers in other settings. They are also less likely to assume that deaf students' limited English skills are a barrier to solving word problems. Research involving older students, meanwhile, has indicated that teachers in mainstream classrooms and those in separate classrooms for deaf students have rather different views of what education is all about. Those who teach hearing students generally view the goal of instruction as *information transmission*, a teacher-focused approach aimed at transferring knowledge from teacher to student. Experienced teachers of deaf students, in contrast, tend to have a more student-focused approach to instruction, emphasizing *conceptual change*. Both of these orientations, of course, are a function of teachers' experiences with the students who normally come into their classrooms. The findings thus may help to explain the results of our recent studies showing that in classes with experienced teachers of the deaf, deaf students may learn just as much as their hearing peers even when they start out with less content knowledge.

IMPROVING MATHEMATICS PERFORMANCE BY DEAF CHILDREN

Bringing together research on mathematics instruction and mathematics achievement by deaf children indicates the importance of the two factors described earlier to improving their academic outcomes. One is having teachers who are knowledgeable both in the content area (also true for other subject areas) and in educating deaf students. The other factor is using materials and methods that build on students' strengths and accommodate their needs. Thus, for example, we need to recognize and take advantage of deaf students' visual-spatial orientations while compensating for their lack of experience and confidence in solving mathematical problems.

An intervention program aimed at improving deaf preschoolers' understanding of basic mathematical concepts that includes all of these elements was recently created by researchers at Oxford University. Teachers are trained in a curriculum that gives children visual representations of the relations between the various parts of math problems while also encouraging use of their visual-spatial abilities.

Diagrams and illustrations represent the visual information deaf children need to understand problems, while emphasis on the various problem components fosters an analytical approach to problem solving. In one study, the majority of deaf children improved significantly in their mathematics test scores after 1 year with the curriculum, and teachers reported that students enjoyed the activities. Perhaps most important, children began generating drawings spontaneously during problem solving, indicating *transfer of the training* from the math program to other subjects.

It is not entirely clear which aspects of this program led to the positive outcomes, but both cognitive and motivational factors were probably involved. That is, use of visual representations supported children's intuitions about mathematical and number concepts while it increased their interest in and enjoyment of mathematics. These advantages were also likely supported by the teachers' behavior, reflecting the benefits of their training with the curriculum and their own increased motivation as children's interest and progress reinforced their activities. It also is important that the kinds of problems emphasized in the program require reasoning and problem solving, rather than simple concrete manipulations of objects or pictures (such as counting or arranging them in a particular pattern). In fact, recent research has shown visual-spatial displays that represent schematic, relational aspects of a problem are more helpful and more predictive of success than simple pictures (see Figure 10.1). This program thus builds on deaf children's visual-spatial strengths while emphasizing the development of relational problem-solving approaches.

The motivational aspect of the aforementioned program is an important one, although motivation is not an area that has been researched much with regard to the education of deaf children. Given how difficult mathematics is for them, it would not be surprising if they found it uninteresting or even actively resisted math-related activities. Of course, many hearing children resist math-related activities too, but we need to acknowledge that deaf children tend to be farther behind in their math achievement and have greater need of explicit instruction in the reasoning and critical thinking skills associated with it. Hearing children gain a lot of their mathematical knowledge through overhearing conversations, interacting with

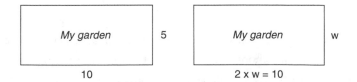

FIGURE 10.1 Which diagram is a better math teaching tool?

diverse other children and adults, and noticing the relations between what they see and what they hear. Math instruction and the encouragement of problem-solving activities more generally offer opportunities for young deaf children to gain many of the skills that they might miss due to the lesser availability of incidental learning. When teachers are aware of deaf children's learning styles and tendencies, they can shape their instructional methods to be more accessible and more interesting for those students. Still to be discovered is what it is that effective math teachers of the deaf do that allows poorly prepared deaf students to learn as much as hearing peers. We are making progress in that regard, but we still have a long way to go.

In addition to motivation, we also could discuss the importance of effective communication between teachers and students during mathematics instruction. By this point, however, we assume that this issue is obvious, and we do not need to belabor the point. In our own work involving deaf college students' learning of mathematics, we have found that regardless of whether instructors are deaf or hearing, students taught by experienced instructors of the deaf make greater gains than those taught by mainstream instructors.[2] Some of this may be due to student motivation, as surveys of deaf students have found that they prefer deaf teachers and teachers who sign for themselves, and we obtain the same results when teachers of the deaf use sign language interpreters. More centrally, however, they value teachers who are clear communicators, regardless of their sign language fluency or mode of communication.

On the basis of findings from our own research, we are coming to believe that one of the greatest strengths of seasoned teachers of the deaf is that they have learned through experience how best to interact with their deaf students, regardless of whether that is through sign language, spoken language, or both. Similarly, contrary to the assumptions of many educators, there is no evidence that story problems are any more difficult for deaf students than straightforward computational problems, and so difficulty in mathematics cannot be ascribed to reading or English skills per se. There is nothing special about communication when it comes to teaching or learning mathematics; it is just as important as in any other subject. Next we will move on to issues associated with the rooms where instruction takes place.

FINAL WORDS

Let us briefly summarize what we know about mathematics achievement by deaf children. While deaf preschoolers may demonstrate basic concepts about number and quantity, by the time they enter school they already lag behind hearing peers in number operations and conceptual understanding of mathematics. This situation is partly language related, because most of them are likely to have limited communication about mathematical concepts with their parents and fewer opportunities to acquire such knowledge through incidental learning. After entering school, delays in language development, the relative lack of exposure to real-world problem solving (both incidentally and in classrooms), and inadequate teacher preparation in mathematics frequently lead to greater lags in mathematics achievement relative to hearing peers and larger individual differences within the population of deaf children. Limitations in language fluency and accessibility often impede access to instruction as well as to text, and deaf children often lack age-appropriate command of the vocabulary of mathematics.

Surveys of teachers and classroom observations indicate that relatively little class time with deaf children is devoted to problem-solving activities, although teachers certified in mathematics and those with training in mathematics instruction are more likely to encourage analytically oriented approaches to problem solving among their students. Such conceptually oriented instruction contrasts with the efforts of some teachers of the deaf to simplify math by making it concrete and easily captured by drawings and diagrams (similar to what some do in reading). Deaf students do show strong visual-spatial abilities, but we are only beginning to learn how best to take advantage of that strength. As a result, and also as a reflection of metacognitive issues discussed previously, deaf students frequently do not apply their visual-spatial skills in problem-solving situations in which it would be helpful or necessary. In particular, given the demonstrated advantage held by deaf individuals in the generation and manipulation of mental images, we need to develop strategies that allow them to use such skills in relating multiple pieces of information and identifying relationships (see Box 10.2).

In addition to mathematics-specific factors, deaf students often lack confidence and motivation with regard to mathematics (and academics more generally). Lacking confidence in their ability to perform and without high expectations on the part of parents and teachers, students may not seriously commit themselves to solving problems in school or elsewhere. The situation is compounded by adults frequently being overcontrolling and overly directive of deaf children, leading them to become *instrumentally dependent*, that is, frequently looking to others for help and support rather than attempting to solve problems themselves (see Chapter 4). Deaf children sometimes also have been found to have difficulties in maintaining attention in some tasks, particularly when they involve multiple operations or logical steps. This may partly reflect a lack of strong foundational concepts and basic information processing skills. Although it is not clear how much these characteristics are attributable to differences in learning styles or cognitive processing between them and hearing students, it is clear that modifications in curricula and in teaching strategies

BOX 10.2
USING VISUAL-SPATIAL STRATEGIES IN PROBLEM SOLVING

Deaf students generally display better visual-spatial skills than hearing students, but they have to learn when those skills will be useful. Consider the following word problem in Figure:

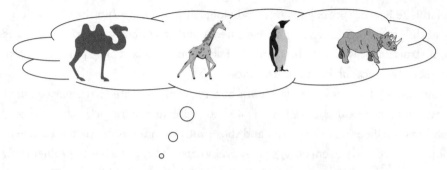

There are four cages in a zoo. Each cage contains one animal. The giraffe is to the right of the camel. The penguin is to the right of the giraffe, And the rhinoceros is to the right of the penguin.

Is the penguin to the right of the camel?
Is the giraffe to the right of the camel?

When hearing children read this description, they form a kind of mental image or mental model that preserves the order of the animals (the same can be done with size, intelligence, and other characteristics). Because of the increasing distances between animals in the mental image, they are faster in answering the first question than the second question. When deaf children read the description, they are less likely to put the animals together into a single image, and their response times for the two questions are, therefore, about the same (this is how we know they are not using an image). Yet deaf individuals generally are faster and more accurate than hearing individuals in generating such images! Apparently, we need to teach deaf children explicitly when and how to use their visual-spatial advantage.

are required if deaf children are to develop to their potential in the important areas of mathematics achievement. When such accommodations are made, they are seen to learn as much in mathematics classes as their hearing peers.

THE DEAF EDUCATION CLASSROOM

PREVIOUS CHAPTERS HAVE been concerned primarily with how deaf children learn, with suggestions for supporting learning wherever possible. Most of the information and ideas about improving instruction came from the fields of developmental and cognitive psychology, focusing on the ways in which deaf children interact with people, things, and knowledge. In this chapter, we focus on the classroom, considering how the *place* and the *people in it* influence deaf children's learning.

If you were to look at the current scientific literature in deaf education about educational placement and practice as well as that concerning teaching and learning, you would find far less information than you might expect on how best to structure classrooms and instruction for deaf children. One reason for that is that there is far less research on how to teach deaf students than there is on how they learn.

We have already noted that in some settings, deaf students learn as much as their hearing classmates even if they come into the classroom with less content knowledge. Those findings have been consistent regardless of whether those teachers are signing for themselves or utilizing sign language interpreters, and they contrast with findings from mainstream classrooms, even when the interpreters are the same. In the mainstream classrooms that have been studied, deaf students generally have been found to learn less than their hearing peers. That research, however, has focused primarily on issues such as the language of instruction, the

effects of instruction through interpreting or *real-time text* (see later discussion), and student characteristics such as use of cochlear implants, language skills, and family and educational backgrounds. We have just begun to try to determine what exactly it is that skilled teachers of the deaf do differently than equally skilled teachers of hearing students that makes for such a distinction.

What we do know from our own research and that of others—with a little common sense thrown in—is that it is the teachers and other students in classrooms with deaf students, together with the support services provided and parental involvement, that will primarily determine the eventual academic outcomes. No curriculum or individualized education program can be expected to lead to academic success unless the students are appropriately prepared, teachers know how to teach deaf students, and those students receive support and encouragement from their parents. In the following sections, we look at how those pieces of the academic puzzle (hopefully) come together in educating deaf students. Both a challenge and an opportunity in this regard is the diversity of educational models in deaf education, as well as the diverse characteristics and skills of the students they are intended to serve. Unfortunately, most families do not have the opportunity to choose from two or three educational placements for their deaf child, because they often are pushed into one that is locally available and administratively convenient. Only by being armed with knowledge of their alternatives can parents make informed choices and push for educational services that will help their child succeed.

OPTIONS IN DEAF EDUCATION PROGRAMMING

Educational options for deaf and hard-of-hearing students include regular or *main-stream* classrooms, separate classrooms within local public schools, and separate *center programs,* including schools for the deaf, that are specifically designed for deaf students. There is considerable variation within these categories. For example, some programs, like the Willie Ross School for the Deaf in Massachusetts, own or rent classrooms in local public schools where deaf students are taught by teachers of the deaf but have the option of walking down the hall (with a sign language interpreter, if appropriate) and being part of mainstream classrooms. Other center programs offer the opportunity for deaf children to take some of their classes at a local regular school (*partial mainstreaming*). Some even offer *reverse mainstreaming,* a model in which hearing children come to the center programs for part of the school day.

What we have referred to so far as *mainstream classrooms* also vary widely. In some contexts, *mainstreaming* refers to settings in which deaf and hard-of-hearing students attend classes in regular classrooms but receive support services (like hearing aid adjustment, tutoring, and counseling) in a separate resource room. In other classrooms, often referred to as *inclusive* classrooms, those services come to the child. And, of course, there is everything in between.

At least within the United States, students in mainstream classrooms frequently are the only deaf or hard-of-hearing children in their classes, and they may be the only ones in the entire school or school system. In situations like that, teachers and school administrators may know little about educating deaf students, and they will be unaware of how much support students need (this is where parent advocacy comes in). Some students will be expected to function without any support services, while others have educational interpreters or other support personnel (with varying levels of skill and experience). They may be visited periodically by an *itinerant teacher of the deaf,* or they may be in a *congregated setting* with several other deaf and hard-of-hearing peers as well as hearing students.

At one extreme, some deaf students have hearing teachers who had never met a deaf student before; at the other, some have deaf teachers who have taught deaf or hard-of-hearing students for many years. Frequently, deaf and hard-of-hearing students find themselves in different educational placements at different times during their schooling, sometimes transferring between mainstream schools and center schools more than once. In addition to having to make new friends in a new school—difficult enough if you are not deaf—there is variability (if not confusion) created by differences across schools for supporting sign language and spoken language, differing availability of technologies to support hearing and visual learning, and the likelihood that as children move to different programs they will encounter different communication practices in each placement. All of this not only creates a challenge for children's learning and families' decision making, but it makes it difficult for investigators to find out what works and what doesn't in educating deaf children.

ASSESSMENT AND CLASSROOM PLACEMENT

Educational services typically rely on assessment by a team of professionals working with parents to determine which classroom or educational setting is likely to be best for a deaf child. The team of professionals may include a curriculum specialist, school psychologist, audiologist, speech–language pathologist, and sign language specialist. It should be mentioned here that no matter how skilled or experienced these professionals are, the decision of which placement might be appropriate for any individual child is more of an art than a science. There are pros and cons for all placements, and one can say the same about schools for hearing children: Some schools are better than others, and some simply are better suited to particular children. Parents are frequently intimidated by the school placement process (who wouldn't be?) but they know their child best, and ultimately the decision is up to them. In cases where parents and school systems cannot agree on an acceptable solution, mediators often are available to act in the legal and best interests of the child while recognizing possible limitations in resources.

A frequent problem in determining the most appropriate placement for deaf or hard-of-hearing children is the lack of assessment tools. Sometimes those tools are available but are not used; at other times, even when they are used, the results are ignored in decision making. There are no standardized tests on the market that can predict which children will benefit from one kind of school program or another, just as there are no tests that can predict who will benefit most from a cochlear implant or which children will find sign language or spoken language most supportive for learning. The best we can do is to assess various skills that students will need in school if they are to be successful and make decisions on that basis.

In North America, there also are no standardized tests available to evaluate children's American Sign Language (ASL) skills, although there are a variety of tools for evaluating spoken language. This does not indicate a bias against signed language; rather, it reflects the fact that speech assessments are given to hearing as well as deaf children, whereas sign language assessments typically are only given to deaf children. The relatively small number of deaf children means that it is economically difficult to develop, evaluate, and pilot test a sign language assessment enough times to demonstrate its accuracy (*validity*) and ability to give consistent results over time and across settings (*reliability*). Some schools provide signed language assessments for their students, usually tests they have developed themselves or adapted from one created for research purposes. We thus have a situation in which a speech–language pathologist may be able to describe a deaf child's spoken language skills (or lack thereof), but the assessment team may be completely ignorant of the child's full *language* skills.

School psychology evaluations can show the strengths and weaknesses of deaf and hard-of-hearing students in various academic and social domains, but the resulting profiles typically do not indicate which type of educational placement is best for a particular student. They usually show children's general level of cognitive abilities (intelligence) and where they stand compared to hearing or deaf children of the same age and grade (see Chapter 6). Those evaluations also indicate whether a student has any particular learning, behavioral, or emotional challenges. When the school psychologist has experience with deaf children, the evaluation also can be useful for showing what extra attention a deaf or hard-of-hearing student might need in the classroom and informing those involved about accompanying strengths.

CLASSROOM DIVERSITY

The classroom today is not the same as classrooms of a generation or two ago, even for hearing children. In Chapter 2, we described the shift in deaf education over the past several decades from most students being in schools for the deaf to most being in mainstream classrooms with their hearing peers. This is generally true with regard to most students with special education needs. In Chapter 7, we discussed the issue of classroom challenges when children come from families with varying home languages, a factor that may be accompanied by varying cultural values. In today's world, the classrooms in many countries are more likely than ever to include variations in socioeconomic status, race, ethnic background, nationality, religion, language experience, and disability. Variation may be even greater in programs and schools for deaf children, both because there is greater variation within the population of deaf children and because with fewer children, differences among individual children are likely to be greater. This diversity is one of the biggest challenges facing teachers today.

One of the most obvious sources of diversity in classrooms with multiple deaf students is language. Imagine a classroom that includes a fifth grader who acquired native fluency in ASL from her deaf parents, where the other deaf students have only recently started learning to sign and are perhaps joined by a boy with a cochlear implant who was not developing enough speech and hearing skills to continue to be in a mainstream classroom. The teacher of these 11- to 12-year-olds is expected to teach content matter, do everything else that a classroom teacher needs to do during the day, and at the same time facilitate students' language development—all when they are at different levels. He must teach the new boy language (perhaps his first accessible classroom language) so he can learn how to learn. He must continue to teach all of the students language skills and vocabulary as well. This includes teaching English to a group of students whose reading levels might range from a first-grade equivalent to a sixth-grade equivalent. If this seems an almost impossible situation, it is one all too familiar to teachers of the deaf, and the story would be much the same if the children primarily utilized spoken language.

Compared to when the baby boomers were in school, one of the greatest contributors to classroom diversity for teachers of the deaf (but also for teachers in mainstream classrooms) is the greater likelihood of having students who have learning, mental, and physical disabilities. For teachers to work effectively with these students, they should have had training and supervision in teaching students with multiple challenges, an area in which we have already seen there is little research to guide instruction. Teachers who have gone through a teacher of the deaf training program in the last 20 years likely will have had a relevant course, but they might not have received supervised practice or even observed classrooms including such children.

Working with deaf students who have disabilities places additional demands on a teacher of the deaf, requiring more individual time in a setting that is perhaps least able to afford it. At least those teachers will have some idea of "where the students are" and what accommodations will be necessary to support their learning. In the mainstream classroom, many teachers are totally at a loss. It is not unusual for such teachers to tell a sign language interpreter the deaf child is her responsibility, even though it is unlikely that the interpreter has any education training at all. Other teachers have sufficient experience and confidence to be able to be more inclusive and creative, making the classroom comfortable for all students.

THE CLASSROOM

In Chapter 5, we talked about deaf and hard-of-hearing children as visual learners. In that context, we noted that the greater sensitivity of deaf students to movement in their peripheral vision can lead to greater distractibility in the classroom. Consistent with research looking at the visual-spatial abilities of deaf children, we suggested that classroom seating be organized so that all children are facing the teacher (and preferably not looking out on the playground). Open-landscape classrooms that have small groups working with teachers or teacher aides (see later discussion) in different areas are likely to be as visually disruptive as multiple noisy working groups would be for hearing students. If such areas have already been constructed, room dividers can be set up, low enough so that teachers can see over them. Alternatively, small groups can be arranged so that the children in each group are facing corners of the room, while teachers and aides are all facing toward the center.

Careful consideration of classroom acoustics is also important in helping children maintain visual attention. Children's voices, chairs scraping on the floor, and other normal classroom sounds tend to be relatively high in frequency. Carpeting, curtains, and other materials that absorb rather than reflect sound can help prevent hearing aids and cochlear implants being bombarded with irrelevant sounds, thus improving communication and reducing distractions. Things as simple as putting tennis balls on the legs of schoolroom chairs can be helpful modifications.

DEAF EDUCATION PROFESSIONALS

Regardless of whether they are in a mainstream setting or in a deaf classroom, deaf children will work with a variety of deaf education professionals throughout their educational careers.

Teachers of the Deaf

Not all deaf and hard-of-students are lucky enough to have trained teachers of the deaf, often referred to as *ToDs* (tee-oh-deez).[1] ToDs are specifically trained in graduate programs that focus on deaf education, receiving hours of supervised teaching with deaf and hard-of-hearing students. To be considered a ToD (rather than someone who just happens to teach deaf children), one must pass state licensure as a specialist in deaf education and, increasingly, a content area of specialization as well (mathematics, science, etc.). In the United States, license or certification requirements vary from state to state, as do their exams, but some countries have national requirements and examinations. ToDs have a wealth of knowledge about how deaf and hard-of-hearing children learn and how to teach them, although it is only recently that programs have started teaching courses on "the psychology of deaf learners" or others that recognize and explain cognitive differences between deaf and hearing children.

One challenge for both mainstream and separate programs that include deaf students is the shortage of ToDs. Programs often have to hire teachers while they are working on their training/certification or have an area of specialization different from the one in which they are expected to teach. Despite this shortage, teacher of the deaf training programs around the United States are closing because there are fewer classrooms dedicated to deaf children, and fewer graduate students are applying to those programs. In difficult economic times, itinerant teachers are given larger caseloads, and this often drives them from the field, resulting in an even greater shortage. Other teachers leave the field because of the greater stress and limited resources associated with teaching deaf students with diverse needs. As rewarding as deaf education can be, without the right tools and with students who have so many challenges, teachers of the deaf burn out at a much higher rate than teachers of hearing children.

As described earlier, ToDs often have to work in classrooms that are linguistically more diverse than other classrooms. They usually have specialized in at least one form of visual communication: spoken communication (moving their lips clearly and unambiguously), some form of signed English, cued speech, or ASL. Given the variability in ToDs' communication skills and students' language skills, perhaps it is not surprising that there is no evidence indicating that one mode of communication in the classroom leads to better learning than any other. Numerous studies with students at the college level have found that deaf and hard-of-hearing students learn essentially the same amount regardless of whether ToDs are deaf or hearing, signing for themselves or using interpreters. When they have been signing for themselves, similar results have been obtained regardless of whether they were using ASL, a form of signed English, or simultaneous communication (see Chapter 4). One unpublished study has found that deaf children learned more when they received direct instruction from a deaf ToD compared to students in a mainstream setting with a hearing teacher and an educational interpreter. However, differences were found only for some lessons and not others, and the ToD took twice as long to give the same lessons as the mainstream teacher. The cause of the differences that were observed between the deaf ToD and the mainstream teacher therefore are unclear and may or may not be obtained if the experiment were repeated with different teachers.

Communication aside, studies at the college level have consistently shown that deaf students do better in the classroom with ToDs than with mainstream teachers.

The general finding is that when students' *gains* are measured, that is, how much they learn given where they started, deaf students learn as much as their hearing classmates. These findings have been attributed to experienced ToDs being more aware of their students' cognitive strengths and needs. In a recent study mentioned earlier, however, experienced ToDs and equally experienced mainstream teachers were found to have rather different views of their educational goals. Mainstream teachers indicated that their goal was the transmission of information from them to their students, and their approaches to teaching reflected a teacher-oriented view of instruction ("After all, it's my classroom"). Experienced ToDs, in contrast, reported viewing their instructional goal as promoting cognitive change in their students, a student-oriented focus on bringing deaf students to a broader understanding of content and its relevance to their lives ("After all, I'm here for them!").

Teacher attitudes alone are unlikely to fully explain differences in learning with experienced ToDs compared to mainstream teachers, just as students' beliefs that they learn more from deaf teachers and teachers who sign for themselves actually have little effect on learning. Attitude and motivation on both parts, however, clearly are important, and we are just beginning to study what it is that teachers and students do differently in mainstream and separate classrooms that leads to differing academic outcomes.

Itinerant Teachers

Itinerant teachers who work with deaf children are usually ToDs who work for a school district or authority. They do not really have a home school. They travel to different schools within the district that have deaf or hard-of-hearing students in mainstream settings. Itinerant teachers provide consultation to mainstream students' teachers who may have no training or experience working with deaf or hard-of-hearing students. They also work directly with deaf and hard-of-hearing students on a one-to-one basis to provide instruction in specific subjects, to provide tutoring, and to provide other services described in the child's Individualized Educational Program (IEP).

Itinerant teachers have to coordinate services with other members of the deaf or hard-of-hearing students' educational team such as the educational interpreter, speech–language pathologist, and educational administrators at the student's school. In addition to working with students on academic content and skills, itinerant teachers may provide deaf students with social-emotional counseling and support, helping them to feel more comfortable in mainstream classrooms.

Teacher Aides

Some deaf and hard-of-hearing students in mainstream settings have a teacher aide who works with the classroom teacher. The teacher aide might be exclusively designated to work with the deaf or hard-of-hearing student(s) but not their hearing classmates. A teacher aide might be assigned to a classroom for various reasons. Perhaps the deaf or hard-of-hearing child does not have enough language skills to be in the classroom without the aide. Perhaps the child has difficulty following what's going on in the classroom and needs the aide to point out where to look or to elaborate classroom content. In some cases, the teacher aide might be the only one in the classroom who has sign language skills, even if she is not an educational interpreter. The teacher aide might have individualized lessons for the deaf or hard-of-hearing student and provide instruction in the classroom just to that one student.

Deaf and hard-of-hearing students in separate classrooms also may have teacher aides for much the same reasons. In addition, because of the diverse needs and skills of deaf students in such classrooms, the ToD simply may need help in handling all of the academic, language, and behavioral needs of the students. In some schools, deaf teacher aides are hired specifically to increase the amount of sign language in the classroom and provide deaf role models for students. Deaf teacher aides are not only found in deaf classrooms, however. We know of one elementary school that provides a deaf teacher aide in a mainstream classroom with an educational interpreter. Since the educational interpreter does not have a role in teaching, the deaf aide works on a one-on-one basis with a deaf student to help her learn and adjust to the mainstream setting. The deaf teacher aide also provides feedback to the educational interpreter and sometimes elaborates when interpretations are complicated.

Sign Language Specialists

Over the past decade, more deaf children have been receiving services from sign language specialists. Their job duties are similar to speech–language pathologists except they do not focus on the child's speech development but the child's signed language development. A part of their role might be assessing deaf and hard-of-hearing students' signed language skills and reporting on the progress of their development. This is a growing profession that is much needed. Some deaf education graduate programs offer a track for sign language specialists or sign language teachers to work in the K-12 setting. Most professionals who work as sign language specialists, however, do not have formal training in that area. They often are ToDs with excellent signed language skills who might have some experience in sign language instruction to hearing adults and/or some signed language linguistics knowledge.

As mentioned in Chapter 4, the vast majority of deaf and hard-of-hearing children do not have deaf or native signing parents themselves. Hearing parents often do not learn a signed language fast enough to be a good language model for their child. While ToDs can serve as model signers (as can some deaf and hard-of-hearing peers), ToDs need to focus on teaching the curriculum, not language. The utilization of sign language specialists enables one-to-one (and group) attention to deaf and hard-of-hearing children's sign language development, including vocabulary, grammar, sign language literacy, and use of sign language in different discourse settings. Sign language specialists are especially important in bilingual programs that operate under the theoretical assumption that the acquisition of a signed language will facilitate and accelerate the acquisition of a second language such as English.

Educational Interpreters

Some sign language interpreters work exclusively with deaf students and teachers in educational settings. Interpreter training programs run from 2 to 4 years, and typically assume that trainees already have good signing skills. Interpreter training not only brings students' sign skills to a higher level, but it teaches them how to take information from either sign language or spoken language and put it into the other, recognizing the diversity of deaf individuals and the situations in which they will be working.

Not all interpreter training programs have educational interpreting components. Without such specialized training, interpreters are unlikely to understand the needs of deaf children and be able to optimize their academic support. Some deaf students therefore have to depend on individuals who are unqualified and are unable even to give them full access to classroom instruction and discussion. Less than half of the states in the United States require educational interpreters to receive certification, indicating that they have at least the minimal necessary skills to interpret; and less than half of working interpreters are certified.

Real-Time Text (Captioning)

A relatively new trend in deaf education is to provide students with *real-time text* (or *speech-to-text*) services in mainstream settings. Typically, an operator in the classroom with the deaf student produces text on a computer screen as it is spoken by the teacher and other students using a stenographic machine (Communication Access Real-Time Translation or CART), automatic speech recognition (C-Print), or a standard keyboard. Studies have found that high school students remember more from a class supported by real-time text than by sign language interpreters. Other studies have found no differences among college students, and the only one we know of involving younger children found real-time text just as effective as signing by a deaf teacher.

In mainstream classrooms, real-time text is frequently promoted as a less expensive alternative to interpreting that also can provide greater access to the classroom for some students. Students certainly say that they understand more from real-time captioning than from interpreting, but they also think they understand more sign language than they actually do, and we still need to determine which students find greater benefits in which settings. In particular, real-time text would appear to present some real challenges for deaf students because its speed is likely to exceed their reading abilities. Even controlling for reading level, deaf students have been found to learn less from video captioning than hearing peers, apparently because of differences in background knowledge and information processing. One advantage of speech-to-text services, however, is that students can have a full transcript of what was said in the classroom (or at least everything the captionist was able to catch).

The use of both real-time text and visual displays in the classroom may create a situation in which deaf students essentially are expected to be looking in two places at the same time. A similar situation may be created by classrooms that include both an interpreter and textual/pictorial displays, potentially forcing deaf students to focus on one or the other at different times. Even without a third source of visual information (e.g., slides or computer screens), students in such situations risk losing the thread of a lecture, because the different information sources will be out of synch, and they usually will be unable to predict which source is more important at any given time.

As long as we are on the subject, it may be worth pointing out the importance of teachers using captioned videos. The majority of video intended for children is now available in captioned format, often with linguistically edited captions to make them more accessible for younger children. Even in classrooms with educational interpreters, captioned videos are important so that deaf and hard-of-hearing children do not have to divide their attention across large distances.

FINAL WORDS

Research cannot tell us which placement is best for an individual deaf or hard-of-hearing student, and we know that there is no one placement that will be best for all of them. There are adolescents who grew up hearing and suddenly began losing some of their hearing, and thus they might require minimal services. There are deaf students who would be best taught in a classroom with deaf peers and in an environment that uses signed language. There is no evidence that schools which emphasize spoken language are better than schools that use a signed language, or vice versa.

It is very hard to study the effects of different educational placements. Many schools do not let researchers test their students if the aim of their study is to measure the effectiveness of their program. Even when a school does grant permission, the deaf students usually will have come from mixed educational backgrounds. Teachers vary a lot, too, in their experience and knowledge with regard to deaf students and in their communication and language skills.

So we are left with what we believe based on what we know. As we mentioned in Chapter 4, we know that signed language does not interfere with learning a spoken language and development but might actually help it. Chapter 6 pointed out that deaf and hard-of-hearing students rely on vision more than do hearing students for learning and that they need to be in an environment that fosters visual learning with teachers who know how to present information visually. Finally, we know that deaf and hard-of-hearing students report being happier and having more friends when they are in educational settings that include other students who are like them, rather than all hearing students. For those who are in mainstream classrooms, social opportunities can be created with afterschool groups, clubs, and programming organized specifically for students who use sign language, cochlear implants, or have some other characteristic or interest in common. Going to school is not just about academics, and parents and teachers need to ensure that their youngsters are thriving in all age-appropriate activities.

12

WHERE DO WE GO FROM HERE?

THIS CHAPTER IS intended to put differences between deaf and hearing children and differences among deaf children into a somewhat larger context. As we have indicated in previous chapters, we believe that a broader and more flexible understanding of deaf learners is important to improving their educational and personal success. There are still misunderstandings and misconceptions about what it means to be deaf, however, and well-meaning do-gooders in various social, academic, and administrative positions still sometimes create as many hurdles to success as they remove.

A JOURNEY OF 1,000 MILES BEGINS WITH A SINGLE STEP

From the 1960s to the 1990s, arguments raged in our field concerning whether there was a *psychology of deafness*. Essentially, the question was whether being deaf fundamentally changes the way that an individual interacts with the world in terms of perception, cognition, and learning. Perhaps surprisingly for readers of this book, most people in the field argued "no." But that was a time when the most frequently noted differences between deaf and hearing people were deaf children's academic difficulties, and there was a broad view in society of deaf individuals as "second-class citizens" when it came to language and intelligence; deaf and hard-of-hearing people were therefore perceived as doomed to be illiterate, dependent on others,

and under- or unemployed. As we have explained in the previous chapters, studies have now given us a better understanding of why deaf children often struggle in school. While frequently lagging behind their hearing peers, their academic challenges have little to do with hearing status and much more to do precisely with how they perceive, think about, and interact with the world as visual learners who have varying amounts of auditory input. And these factors are as much about the parents and teachers as they are about children.

Although the negative view of the academic potential of deaf children frequently led people to argue against the idea that there might be a psychology of deafness, at its most basic level that is exactly what we have been saying in the previous chapters: Deaf children are not hearing children who can't hear. With the recognition of signed languages as true languages in the 1960s, things began to change. Researchers started to explore relations among communication, social interaction, and learning. Today, we recognize that primarily because of language barriers, many deaf children do experience a more limited world than do hearing children, that their interactions with people and information will be somewhat different than their hearing peers, and that these differences may have implications for their academic outcomes. Whether we like it or not, many, if not most deaf children still enter school lagging behind in language skills, knowledge of the world, and other aspects of *school readiness*. Their frequent lack of social maturity interferes with peer interactions both in the classroom and elsewhere, potentially creating further difficulties for school success.

THE MORE THINGS CHANGE THE MORE THEY STAY THE SAME

When *universal newborn hearing screening* replaced testing only those babies thought to be at risk of being deaf because of medical or genetic factors, it was expected that early identification would allow children to be channeled into the kinds of programming that best suited their needs. Usually, however, newborn hearing screening is in the hands of people who know about speech and hearing but little about raising and educating deaf children. Partly as a result, most deaf children continue to be placed in spoken language environments, regardless of whether these are the most appropriate. Early intervention and educational programs should be responsible for monitoring deaf children's progress so they can change communication and instructional programming when they are not working. Too often, however, there is a desire to look for the nonexistent "one-size-fits-all" solution and most of the time that initially plays out in the form of oral, mainstream education. When that solution does not work, the tendency is to place blame on the child, the parents, or the teacher rather than on the faulty placement process.

A similar situation occurs in the labeling of children who have received cochlear implants but who have not developed spoken language as "implant failures." Cochlear implantation can be an unpredictable business for any child, and differences in causes of deafness, prior language experience, and cognitive ability as well as educational setting and parental support all are going to affect how much a child is able to benefit from an implant. Just as with deaf children who do not have implants, there has to be ongoing assessment and flexibility in educational programming to avoid deaf children with implants being placed in inappropriate school settings. Unfortunately, we do not yet know how best to educate children with cochlear implants. When they are in mainstream settings, they tend to be treated as though they are hearing students. When they are in separate settings, they are treated as though they are deaf students. As we have seen, they are not exactly either but have specific (and still diverse) strengths and needs that have to be taken into account. Communication methods, instructional methods, and educational placements have to serve the needs of individual students. To the extent that they do not, it is the system that fails, not the child.

THERE ARE DIFFERENCES AND THEN THERE ARE DIFFERENCES

Aside perhaps from their hearing, most deaf and hearing children are born with the same physical and psychological potentials. Differences in their early environments and experience, however, affect both behavior and brain development. Children who have less informal communication with their parents, for example, are going to have smaller vocabularies and thus even more limited communication and interactions with others. When there is less access to communication in the family, there is also less incidental learning of both social and cognitive skills. At the same time, deaf children may be more aware of people and physical characteristics of their environments and more sensitive to changes in them. All of these relationships usually yield quite small differences and vary widely across individuals. We do not mean to suggest that any of them are "all or none." Nor is it the case that the results we do observe have to be either positive or negative. They may just be different.

One example of this balance mentioned earlier is deaf children's greater sensitivity to events outside of their central field of vision. This ability is *biologically adaptive*, because it helps deaf children to attend to possible sources of danger, to other individuals who are seeking their attention, and to environmental events that lead to incidental learning. But while deaf children's peripheral vision is helpful, it also makes them prone to visual distraction from activities going on around them. Recognition of such differences compared to hearing children can be of practical help in the design and arrangement of classrooms and theoretically helpful in understanding the foundations of deaf children's learning in both formal and informal situations. At the same time, recent classroom studies have shown that deaf students who are native signers, later signers, or users of spoken language do not differ from hearing students in their ability to use information presented outside of their central visual field. They know that something is happening out there and can shift their visual attention faster than hearing students, but they cannot process or use that information unless they do so—possibly missing what is right in front of them. Such findings do not make the earlier results any less interesting or less important, but they do help to clarify the notion of *visual learning*. They also emphasize the need for more research on the visual learning experiences of deaf students and how they affect academic achievement.

A similar example can be found in memory studies we described in Chapters 7 and 8. Early research showed poorer memory performance of deaf adults and children and concluded that it was due to poor language, poor education, or lower intelligence. Later studies, however, showed that deaf children simply do not have (or maybe do not know when to use) some of the memory strategies that hearing children have. We also now know that memory is influenced by children's use of spoken language versus sign language, so recall performance will differ depending on both the child's language skills and the nature of the to-be-remembered material.

Unfortunately, researchers' acceptance of cognitive differences has not led to any obvious changes in educational practice. In part, this is because few researchers have

The educational needs of deaf and hard-of-hearing students are evolving. The reasons for this evolution are varied but primarily are rooted in the growing heterogeneity of the students. Earlier detection of hearing loss through universal newborn screening, the increasing frequency of pediatric cochlear implantation, and advances in digital hearing aids are just three factors affecting the population of children with hearing loss. These examples also represent new opportunities to enhance both early intervention and educational programming for deaf and hard-of-hearing children— opportunities that promise to significantly enhance their academic outcomes. At the same time, the growing diversity in the needs of these children has strained the capacities of existing educational models to satisfy program and curricular requirements. In order to take advantage of the opportunities presented by these advancements and enhance achievement, we need to increase the efficiency and effectiveness of our educational methods.

Dr. Lou Abbate, Chief Executive
Willie Ross School for the Deaf

(From presentation to the United States Department of Education on the reauthorization of IDEA)

made the effort to share their results with parents and teachers, usually preferring to talk to each other. Realizing that memory for sequences may be more challenging for many deaf children compared to hearing children and for deaf children who sign compared to deaf peers who use spoken language should help us to better organize some day-to-day activities occurring in classrooms. Additionally, recognition that children who sign often will have an advantage in processing, imagining, and presumably learning visual-spatial information could be helpful in developing instructional strategies for content that involves a lot of visual information, such as mathematics or science. It may be that skilled and experienced teachers of the deaf take account of such factors during instruction, just as deaf people themselves do. These possibilities are just now beginning to attract attention, however, and with few exceptions, studies have not yet explored how they might improve deaf children's academic outcomes.

There are a number of other differences between deaf and hearing learners that also have direct relevance for the classroom. As we saw in Chapter 8, studies have demonstrated differences in deaf and hearing students' world knowledge, both in how much they have and how it is organized, as well as their approaches to studying and problem solving (*executive functioning* and *metacognition*; see Chapter 6). Until such information is provided in some usable form to early interventionists and parents of young deaf children, deaf children will continue to arrive at school less prepared and with somewhat different learning strategies than most of their (hearing) classmates. They also will continue to be taught by (mainstream) teachers who are not fully aware of the differences in knowledge, language fluency, and learning styles of their deaf and hearing students. Information about deaf learners and how best to educate them, gained by experienced and successful teachers, needs to be passed along to others who can use it in research, the training of future teachers of the deaf, and in their own classrooms.

WHAT WE KNOW AND WHAT WE NEED TO KNOW

By this point, we hopefully have convinced readers that the development and education of deaf children must be considered together rather than separately. In that way, we can better understand and support both the educational needs and the strengths of deaf children in various learning situations. Some deaf children will not need anything different than hearing children, but they may need more of what they do receive to make sure that their knowledge and skills are sufficient for learning in different contexts. Others will need special methods and technologies if they are to compete successfully with their peers. Let us consider two specific areas that help to highlight this issue.

Language

Throughout this book, language has been identified as perhaps the primary issue in educating deaf children. Because of their hearing losses and the early environments in which they are raised, most deaf children enter school without fluency in either spoken or sign language. Newborn hearing screening, early intervention, and cochlear implants are relatively recent advances that have improved this situation, but even deaf children who have had access to those opportunities still tend to lag behind hearing peers in language development as well as in their academic skills. For deaf children to be able to succeed academically they need language: effective communication with their parents and others, fluent language skills to support literacy, and the internal language involved in reasoning and problem solving. When these are missing, deaf children face a variety of challenges that used to be blamed on hearing loss.

Educational and psychological studies have shown that information presented visually and verbally (meaning *in language*, not necessarily *vocally*) together leads to better comprehension, learning, and memory than information presented either visually or verbally alone. Deaf children who have not learned to to combine language and visual learning thus will be at a disadvantage in both incidental and intentional learning. Aspects of development related to effective communication, like vocabulary knowledge and *theory of mind*, therefore frequently are delayed in young deaf children, just as they are in blind children.

Studies have shown that early language development in deaf children of deaf parents follows much the same pattern and occurs at much the same rate as in their hearing peers, so most researchers consider their language development to be "normal." That does not mean, however, that growing up with a signed language is the same as growing up with a spoken language. We have seen in earlier chapters that growing up primarily using sign language has some specific effects on learning and behavior. Actually, it is still not clear how much of those differences are really the result of using a visual-spatial language, rather than the quality and quantity of the language the child is exposed to or other factors. Being educated through a signed language carries its own challenges though, including teachers' sign skills and interpreters' skills and the fact that it often does not map directly onto text in the same way that spoken language does. Deaf children of deaf parents do have cognitive and language advantages relating to how many different individuals they have conversations with (more interactions with adults lead to larger vocabularies). Like other deaf children, however, they often are taught in classrooms that either have other children who have delayed language development (separate classrooms) or teachers who are not familiar with the learning strategies used by deaf, visual learners (mainstream classrooms). Only by understanding the relations among these factors can we take advantage of the strengths that deaf students bring to various learning contexts and accommodate their needs.

It is now clear that deaf children can be effectively educated through sign language, but we still need to ask about the subtle and not-so-subtle implications of their varying degrees of sign language and spoken language fluencies gained and used at home. Parents may be drawn to spoken language because it makes a child seem more similar to his siblings, because it seems to allow for easier parent–child communication, or because perhaps they unconsciously think their beliefs, thoughts, and values can be passed to their child only through their home language. Other parents fear they will not be able to effectively interact with or develop an appropriate attachment with their child if they have to use a new language. Some simply may believe that their child would have a greater success in acquiring their home language than they themselves would in learning a new one. Those feelings are all understandable. Still, there can be no higher educational or social priority than providing a child with consistent exposure to *accessible* language.

Before leaving the issue of language, it is worth restating something that may be obvious: Our distinction between individuals who use spoken language and those who use sign language is only for convenience. Regardless of the hearing status of their parents, children's hearing thresholds, and their educational placements, most deaf students are exposed to both spoken language and sign language. Hard-of-hearing students are in a similar situation. Although most hard-of-hearing students tend to rely more on spoken language than sign language, progressive hearing losses, social pressures, and context frequently result in familiarity with, if not fluency in, sign language.

Characteristics of Deaf Learners That We Cannot and Should Not Ignore

Whether one likes it or not, there is now abundant evidence that a significant proportion of deaf children are affected by learning disabilities and other neurological, physical, or psychological issues. Estimates of learning disabilities among deaf children vary widely, from 5% to near 25%, but it appears generally accepted that medically related factors overall affect 30%–40% of deaf children. Despite the obvious practical challenges for parents and possible academic and social implications for children, it is difficult to determine how much of deaf children's educational outcomes are affected by such factors. Some researchers avoid the issue by conducting research only with deaf children of deaf parents (some of whom may be affected by genetic syndromes that affect hearing). But that is not going to give us the answers to the everyday questions that parents and teachers are asking about how best to educate their children.

Looking back, the shifting focus on particular aspects of deaf children's development is reflected in educational interventions that have come into and gone out of fashion every few years. Yet even now that we know that there are some real differences between deaf and hearing learners, it is far less clear when these are important and what we should do about them. We *assume* that most of the individual differences among deaf children will be irrelevant or only minimally linked to educational progress. Those differences may be interesting to researchers and some might even be useful as we develop a better understanding of how the specific strengths of deaf children might be used to compensate for specific educational challenges. But, until we *know*, we continue to do a disservice to deaf children, their parents, and their teachers.

There are also areas in which deaf children may have advantages, but which have not yet been explored. Better memory for spatial locations by signers, for example, might prove useful in supporting learning in today's multimedia classrooms, where deaf children have to divide their attention between presented visual materials and language. Similarly, deaf children who sign have been shown to have better face recognition abilities than deaf and hearing nonsigners, at least for components of facial expressions that are relevant for sign language. We thus might expect that they would be better at reading interpersonal social-emotional cues. That skill would also be related to *theory of mind* skills and might be used to help deaf children develop better social maturity, even if they interact with fewer peers than hearing children.

In short, it is now evident that there are a variety of differences in the foundations of learning among deaf learners and between deaf and hearing learners. The time has passed for us to be satisfied with such demonstrations. For those of us who are curious about such differences, it is time to study, or at least provide suggestions about, how such findings might be used to improve educational practice. Similarly, teachers, deaf individuals and parents—as well as providers of interpreting, audiological services, and early interventionists—need to be working together to improve educational methods and outcomes. Otherwise, valuable insights into real-world functioning of deaf students will be lost in the search for simple answers to complex questions.

FINAL FINAL WORDS

Being a parent or a teacher of a deaf child may not be easy. Particularly for first-time or younger parents, changes in family life when a child is born take considerable adjustment. Finding out that one's child is different from others or will have special needs can be scary, but having a deaf child will be no less rewarding, less enjoyable, or less exciting than having a hearing child. There are some emotional and practical issues that parents will need to resolve, but hopefully we have shown that they do get resolved, and we move on. Dealing with those matters requires both professional information and sharing of experiences with others who are in similar situations. For parents, such support can come from parent–infant (early intervention) programs and preschools for deaf and hard-of-hearing children within the community as well as from national organizations for the families of deaf children. For teachers and other professionals, such support can come from workshops and various professional development opportunities that focus on the needs of deaf students.

Recognizing that deaf children are in some ways different and in some ways the same as hearing children is an important step for both parents and teachers. As much as we might want them to be like hearing children, forcing deaf children into that mold does them no service and may do them harm. We can have high expectations for deaf children without pretending they are something they are not. If they are to receive support in those areas in which they need it, they must be appreciated in their own right; and we should recognize that they might need more or different educational experiences to derive the same benefits. Similarly, if they are to develop as individuals in areas in which they do not need help, we must try to allow deaf children all of the freedoms and experiences of hearing children without being overly controlling of their behavior either at home or at school. It therefore is important to keep in mind that methods for understanding the abilities of hearing children might not always be appropriate for deaf children. Deaf children are not hearing children who cannot hear, but *differences* should not be equated with *deficiencies*.

The two primary themes of this book have been the need for early and consistent exposure to language and the importance of recognizing cognitive differences between deaf and hearing children. The language and cognitive abilities of deaf children are fundamental to their interactions with people and with the world. Competence (or incompetence) in these areas will be influenced by a wide range of experiences with other deaf adults and children, hearing adults and children, and members of their families. They will be reflected in deaf children's social and educational outcomes. We therefore have placed much of the responsibility for these needs on parents and teachers. We urge them to take active and proactive roles in deaf children's educations. Flexibility, patience, and communication skill are essential for the parents and teachers of any child. Deaf children may require a greater quantity of each of these, but the quality of the stuff is essentially the same.

Notes

CHAPTER 1

1. *Cognition* is the scientific term for *thinking*. As it is used in psychology and other fields—and the way we will use it here—it usually includes mental activities such as memory, perception, and problem solving, in addition to the conscious activity (reflection, consideration) we normally associate with thinking.

CHAPTER 2

1. Being able to *control* for various factors is one of the difficult parts of conducting research. The idea is to attribute results to the characteristic or intervention under investigation, ruling out the possibility that they are caused by something else. This kind of control can be achieved either through experiments involving different groups (for example, comparing children with and without cochlear implants but equal in every other respect) or statistically, by mathematically equating children on factors other than the one under consideration.

2. In some countries, like the Netherlands, there are separate schools for deaf and hard-of-hearing children.

3. The fact that Eskimos and cross-country skiers have many words for snow is the result of snow being important to them. Because of those differences, their children will learn those words and what they refer to. The words do not let them see the differences better than anyone else; the words just label the differences that they notice.

CHAPTER 4

1. Fingerspelling is only used in Hong Kong Sign Language for English words and is not part of HKSL.

2. Although we refer here to signed English, as opposed to ASL, most countries have similar situations (for example, Polish Sign Language and signed Polish).

3. One reason why oral programs tend to be successful it that they often only accept children who appear likely to acquire spoken language. This should not be seen as dishonest, but simply an appropriate effort to help those children most likely to benefit from their methods.

CHAPTER 6

1. Many "baby sign" books do not use real sign language; rather, they use gestures created by their authors. These are no easier to learn than real signs, and thus they seem a waste of time and money when children could be learning a real language, potentially enabling them to converse with others.

CHAPTER 10

1. This is one reason why early intervention programming can be almost as important for deaf children of deaf parents as it is for those of hearing parents.

2. This might seem odd given our earlier description of teachers in mainstream classrooms as better qualified to teach math. But that was about school teachers; this is about university instructors.

CHAPTER 11

1. Yes, we know this should be TsoD, like RBIs should be RsBI, but that's not what people use.

Suggestions for Further Reading

CHAPTER 2

Lang, H. (2011). Perspectives on the history of deaf education. In M. Marschark & P. E. Spencer, (Eds.), *The Oxford handbook of deaf studies, language, and education, Volume 1* (2nd ed.) (pp. 7–17). New York: Oxford University Press.

Raimondo, B. (2010). Legal advocacy for deaf and hard-of-hearing children in education. In M. Marschark and P. E. Spencer (Eds.) *The Oxford handbook of deaf studies, language, and education, Volume 2* (pp. 31–40). New York: Oxford University Press.

CHAPTER 3

Cone, B. (2011). Screening and assessment of hearing loss in infants. In M. Marschark & P. E. Spencer (Eds.), *The Oxford handbook of deaf studies, language, and education, Volume 1* (2nd ed.) (pp. 439–451). New York: Oxford University Press.

Marschark, M., Rhoten, C., & Fabich, M. (2007). Effects of cochlear implants on children's reading and academic achievement. *Journal of Deaf Studies and Deaf Education, 12,* 269–282.

CHAPTER 4

Gleason, J. B., & Ratner, N. B. (2009). *The development of language* (7th ed.). Boston, MA: Allyn & Bacon/Pearson.

Schick, B. (2011). The development of American Sign Language and Manually Coded English systems. In M. Marschark & P. E. Spencer (Eds.), *The Oxford handbook of deaf studies, language, and education, Volume 1* (2nd ed.) (pp. 229–240). New York: Oxford University Press.

CHAPTER 5

Kisor, H. (2010). *What's that pig outdoors? A memoir of deafness* (2nd ed.) New York: Hill & Wang.

Leigh, I. L. (2010). *A lens on deaf identity*. New York: Oxford University Press.

CHAPTER 6

Marschark, M., & Wauters, L. (2011). Cognitive functioning in deaf adults and children. In M. Marschark, M., & P. E. Spencer (Eds.), *The Oxford handbook of deaf studies, language, and education, Volume 1* (2nd ed.) (pp. 486–499). New York: Oxford University Press.

van Dijk, R., Nelson, C., Postma, A., & van Dijk, J. (2010). Deaf children with severe multiple disabilities: Etiologies, intervention, and assessment. In M. Marschark and P. E. Spencer (Eds.), *The Oxford handbook of deaf studies, language, and education, Volume 2* (pp. 173–191). New York: Oxford University Press.

CHAPTER 7

Hauser, P., & Marschark, M. (2008). What we know and what we don't know about cognition and deaf learners. In M. Marschark & P. C. Hauser (Eds.), *Deaf cognition: Foundations and outcomes* (pp. 439–458). New York: Oxford University Press.

Marschark, M., & Hauser, P. (2008). Cognitive underpinnings of learning by deaf and hard-of-hearing students: Differences, diversity, and directions. In M. Marschark & P. C. Hauser (Eds.), *Deaf cognition: Foundations and outcomes* (pp. 3–23). New York: Oxford University Press.

CHAPTER 9

Mayer, C. (2010). The demands of writing and the deaf writer. In M. Marschark & P. E. Spencer (Eds.), *The Oxford handbook of deaf studies, language, and education, Volume 2* (pp. 144–155). New York: Oxford University Press.

Trezek, B. J., Wang, Y., & Paul, P. V. (2011). Process and components of reading. In M. Marschark & P. E. Spencer (Eds.). *The Oxford handbook of deaf studies, language, and education, Volume 1* (2nd ed.) (pp. 99–114). New York: Oxford University Press.

CHAPTER 10

Kritzer, K. L. (2009). Barely started and already left behind: A descriptive analysis of the mathematics ability demonstrated by young deaf children. *Journal of Deaf Studies and Deaf Education, 14,* 409–421.

Nunes, T., & Moreno, C. (2002). An intervention program for promoting deaf pupils' achievement in mathematics. *Journal of Deaf Studies and Deaf Education, 7,* 120–133.

CHAPTER 11

Schick, B. (2008). A model of learning within an interpreted K-12 educational setting. In M. Marschark & P. C. Hauser (Eds.), *Deaf cognition: Foundations and outcomes* (pp. 351–386). New York: Oxford University Press.

Stinson, M. S., & Kluwin, T. N. (2011). Educational consequences of alternative school placements. In M. Marschark & P. E. Spencer (Eds.), *The Oxford handbook of deaf studies, language, and education, Volume 1* (2nd ed.) (pp. 47–62). New York: Oxford University Press.

Index

Note: Page numbers followed by *b* refer to text boxes. Page numbers followed by *f* indicate figures. Page numbers followed by *n* refer to endnotes.